WITNESSES
BEFORE
DAWN

WITNESSES BEFORE DAWN

William D. Apel

EXPLORING THE MEANING OF CHRISTIAN LIFE

**Dietrich Bonhoeffer
Carlyle Marney
Howard Thurman
Virginia Mollenkott
Elizabeth O'Connor
Dom Helder Camara
Mark Hatfield**

Judson Press ® Valley Forge

Library of Congress Cataloging in Publication Data

Apel, William D.
    Witnesses before dawn.

    Includes bibliographies and index.
    1. Theologians—Biography. 2. Theology—20th century. I. Title.
BT28.A63   280'.092'2 [B]   84-15478
ISBN 0-8170-1031-9

To Jane, Emily, and Paul,
who have taught me
about the grace of God,
and to my parents,
who have always loved me,
even before the dawn.

Contents

Introduction

Now on the first day of the week Mary Magdalene came to the tomb early, while it was still dark, and saw that the stone had been taken away from the tomb.

—John 20:1

Therefore, since we are surrounded by so great a cloud of witnesses, let us also lay aside every weight, and sin which clings so closely, and let us run with perseverance the race that is set before us, looking to Jesus the pioneer and perfecter of our faith. . . .

—Hebrews 12:1-2a

The time just before dawn has always had great significance for followers of Jesus Christ. For century upon century, Christian witnesses have risen before the sun's rise to welcome the beginning of the Lord's day and the celebration of Christ's resurrection. Christian people are accustomed to standing in the dark while looking for the first rays of a new day. From the Christian perspective, darkness cannot last; in fact, it has no sure defense against the brilliance of God's glorious light in Jesus Christ.

Today, Christians as well as others face yet another dawn. All of us, believers and nonbelievers alike, face the beginning of a new century. We are peering out at a new horizon. Some would say we are entering a post-modern world; some would call it the end-times. Whatever the case may be, it is clear that we are on the verge of a new era.

Since Christians have witnessed so many new dawns, those of us who follow the Christ should be prepared for the next turning of events. However, many within the Christian community feel ill-equipped to deal with our emerging future. We seem to have lost our bearings. It may be time to take a reading as to where we are. We need to check our compasses and set a clearer and more definite course for the future. An important way to do this is to examine the life and thought of contemporary Christians who have given serious consideration to the meaning of the Christian life for today's world and for the future.

God has not left us without witnesses. There are brothers and sisters in the faith whose experiences and reflections have given them important insights into authentic Christian existence. We are indeed surrounded by a great cloud of witnesses. These witnesses speak to us of the meaning of the Christian faith for our times and for future times. They are not stained-glass saints; they are flesh and blood human beings like you and me. Perhaps the only real difference between these contemporary witnesses and the rest of us is a matter of degree. Whereas most of us timidly strive to put our faith into action, these "saints" have actually succeeded in doing so. This has been accomplished not because they are morally superior to the rest of us, but because they are more committed than most of us.

This book is, in fact, about commitment. It is about the life and thought of modern Christians whose personal existence has been a testament to the work of God in our day. By examining the biographies of committed Christian people, we hope to un-cover the genuine marks of the Christian life for our journey into God's future. What does it mean to live faithfully in today's world? How can we best prepare for the challenges ahead? These are the kinds of questions we will explore through an investi-gation of the life and thought of a twentieth-century "cloud of witnesses." Each chapter will focus upon the biography of one of our witnesses. Also in each chapter we will concentrate upon a central question of faith for our times and for the emerging future. We will consider how our witness handles this issue of faith, and we will ask ourselves how it is that we too can respond in faithfulness. Our questions range from a consideration of the meaning of Jesus Christ for our present times to an examination of what it means to work for justice and peace for today and tomorrow's world. In the final chapter we will identify some important marks for Christian living based upon what we have learned from our witnesses.

Our witnesses to Christian living are Dietrich Bonhoeffer, Carlyle Marney, Howard Thurman, Virginia Ramey Mollenkott, Elizabeth O'Connor, Dom Helder Camara, and Mark Hatfield. These are not necessarily people that others might chose for the task described; some of these names may be totally unfamiliar to many of us. However, the selection of these people is quite easy to explain. They represent my "cloud of witnesses." These are individuals whose writings—and in some cases, lives—have touched me directly and very deeply. They are movers and shakers; they stir our faith and prick our conscience. I believe these witnesses speak to us of God's activity in today's world.

These witnesses are men and women who have been challenged by the gospel of Jesus Christ. Their lives now stand before us as a challenge to faithfulness. Those who are spiritual seekers, but not Christian, can find kinship with this collection of witnesses because these "saints" have more questions in their lives than answers. The seekers might also connect with these Christian witnesses because the witnesses often border on heresy. They are so intent on demonstrating the relevancy of Christian life that they are not afraid to challenge Christian dogma. Indeed, the witnesses we will read about in this volume share a common conviction that the Christian faith is primarily a way of life and only secondarily a set of doctrines. Those who are believers will also find companionship with the witnesses on these pages. Christians searching for ways to stretch and grow in their faith will certainly meet challenges for Christian maturity here. The paths offered by this "cloud of witnesses" are not easy ones to follow, and the journey can be long and hard.

The witnesses selected to guide us in our investigation of Christian living are not ivory-tower thinkers. They are Christians who have dared to take their faith into the marketplace. They have chosen to live on the cutting edge. This does not mean, however, that our witnesses lack intellectual rigor. Quite the contrary is true; each witness is a theologian in his or her own right, and some are even professional educators. But in each case the center of commitment is located in the life of the individual rather than in some abstract system of ideas. The guides selected for our examination of the Christian life are by definition controversial. They do not represent "consensus-type" Christians. Unlike popular preachers of our electronic media, these witnesses do not seek the lowest common denominator of faith with which all could identify. There is no generic Christianity here. Our witnesses often make radical demands upon our faith and life; they speak much more like prophets than evangelists, although their message at times is very evangelical. Undoubtedly most people will not agree with everything they read in these pages. The activism of some of our witnesses may be troublesome to some. Nevertheless, we will be challenged by each witness to hear the message of God's love and reconciliation, and then we will be asked to respond with our lives. It is true that our witnesses will approach faith in a variety of ways, but we will soon recognize the personal importance they each place upon the life and work of Jesus Christ as "pioneer and perfecter" of our faith.

In the chapters which follow, we will be dealing with Christian witnesses who stand before the dawn. They have placed their vocations, their reputations, and even their lives on the line for the sake of God's emerging light in the world. It is indeed true that those who know the Christian life best are those who live it. The challenge of the gospel is alive because Christians are alive. It is as simple as that. God continues to speak to us today as clearly as God spoke to the ancient Hebrews and early Christians. The activities of God are revealed, as always, through the toils and labors and joys of faithful witnesses. These are women and men who have seen the light dawning for the world in Jesus Christ.

This book is before us, then, as an open invitation to struggle with the meaning of the Christian life for our generation and for the future. It is an invitation to consider the numerous ways in which God continues to lead us through the words and deeds of faithful witnesses. In the work which follows, I accept full responsibility for the interpretation of the lives and thoughts of this particular group of God's faithful witnesses. If in the process, the challenge of faithful living is not heard, then this failure rests upon my shortcomings as a writer.

I could not have completed this work without the support of the many friends who bore with me during the ups and downs that writers experience in an extended project like this. In this regard, Linfield College granted me valuable time for a sabbatical leave which quickened the completion of the present volume. To my partner in dialog and my companion on the journey, Stephen Snyder, I can only hope to return my gratitude for intellectual stimulation by continuing my own journey. I am certainly aware of a vast "cloud of witnesses" who have surrounded my life since its beginning—thanks to my parents, my brother, my teachers, my friends, my colleagues in Student Services at Linfield, and my students both past and present. Most importantly, I wish to thank my most intimate "cloud of witnesses," who teach me about God's love and grace each day of my life—Jane, my life's partner, and Emily Jane and William Paul, our children and our joy.

It is almost a truism, but we *do* hear God's Word in ever new and exciting ways. I believe that those who testify on these pages speak to us in fresh ways concerning the enduring truths of God. The people who make up the "cloud of witnesses" for our consideration of the Christian life deserve our attention because, in my judgment they have persistently asked the "right" questions. Certainly the next generation of witnesses will have something more to add, but for the present I find these witnesses to be quite compelling.

We begin our study with the life and thought of Dietrich Bonhoeffer. Our question will be his question—who is Jesus Christ for us today? This is an excellent place to begin our investigation of the Christian life. We start with the question of Christ, for it is through Christ's eyes that the Christian is called to view all of life. It is in Christ that we are truly witnesses before dawn.

1

DIETRICH BONHOEFFER:
Who Is Christ for Us Today?

And Jesus went on with his disciples to the villages of Caesarea
Philippi; and on the way he asked his disciples, "Who do men
say that I am?"

—Mark 8:27

Who is Jesus Christ? This question has always been on the agenda of Christianity. Each generation of Christians seeks to answer this question to its own satisfaction. Occasionally a voice will speak so clearly of Jesus Christ in one generation that it will be heard in the next. Such is the case with the German pastor and theologian Dietrich Bonhoeffer.

During the rule of Adolf Hitler and the Third Reich, this German citizen dared to question the meaning of Jesus Christ for his time. He was not afraid to place his faith on the line when it became apparent that his country was worshiping a false Messiah. As a prisoner of the Nazi gestapo, he identified his life's concern from behind prison bars: "What is bothering me incessantly is the question what Christianity is, or indeed who Christ really is, for us today."[1]

Bonhoeffer's question is also our question. We cannot come to an understanding of the Christian faith without confronting the question of Jesus Christ. And like Bonhoeffer, we need to be pointed in our questioning. It is one thing to ask who Christ is for all eternity; it is quite another thing to ask who he is for our day and for our unique set of circumstances. With Bon-

hoeffer's help we can learn to ask our questions about Jesus
Christ with a boldness and directness which will bring him alive
for our time and place. Please do not expect easy answers from
Bonhoeffer in relation to the meaning of Jesus Christ, but do
expect a great deal of honesty and authenticity in his inquiry.
Bonhoeffer answered the question of Jesus Christ for himself
through the toils and struggles of his own life. He would suggest
the same for us.

On Becoming a Christian

Dietrich Bonhoeffer was born into an upper-class German
family in 1906. He was one of eight children raised in a happy
and secure home; he had the advantage of an excellent education
in the finest schools. His father was a noted professor of psy-
chiatry, and his mother was the product of a proud Prussian
family whose paternal head had been the chaplain in the court
of William II.

The First World War, beginning in his eighth year, interrupted
Bonhoeffer's childhood. He saw two of his older brothers march
off to war; one brother returned badly wounded, and the other
did not return at all. Living in Berlin, the Bonhoeffer family
heard daily reports from the front. Young Dietrich was deeply
affected by the war. He later recalled, "Death stood at the door
of almost every house."[2] As a result of these early experiences,
he had no taste for war and in his adulthood he embraced a
pacifist position.

Bonhoeffer's religious training was typical of the bourgeois
families of Germany in the first half of the twentieth century.
Christian holidays were observed, but beyond that the family
rarely attended church. Within the home itself Bonhoeffer received religious instruction from his mother. However, when at
the age of seventeen young Dietrich announced that he would
study theology, the entire family was surprised. By the age of
twenty-one he had completed his doctorate, and he finished the
additional work necessary for becoming a university lecturer
shortly thereafter.

Bonhoeffer was bright and well liked by his peers. He was
described by fellow classmates "as capable and assured in man-

ner, stormy in temperament, receptive to new ideas, inclined to indulge in teasing, and endowed with a sharp critical sense, which he was, however, equally prepared to turn towards himself."[3] Yet there is little evidence that Bonhoeffer was a practicing Christian. He had not come to the question of personal faith. Like most of us, he did not pay attention to such matters until he came to a time of personal crisis. Bonhoeffer never said publicly when that turning point came. But something changed in his life. He met the living Christ; he experienced conversion.

Many of us could attest to the power of conversion. Something changes within us; we may not even know precisely when or how it all transpired, but we do know we are now different. This mystery of conversion is described by Bonhoeffer in a letter written to a close friend in the winter of 1935-36. The events he referred to probably took place sometime around 1931. Bonhoeffer confessed:

> I hurled myself into my work in an unchristian and an unhumble manner. . . . Then something else came along, something which has permanently changed my life and its direction. . . . I had often preached, I had seen a lot of the church, I had talked and written about it, but I had not yet become a Christian. (I know that until then I had been using the cause of Jesus Christ to my own advantage. . . .)[4]

Bonhoeffer the theologian had now become Bonhoeffer the Christian. This changed everything.

After becoming a Christian, Bonhoeffer approached his academic work differently. He surprised his students at the University of Berlin in the early 1930s by opening his lectures with prayer. He encouraged his students, for the first time, to gather around him for a fellowship of study and prayer. This broke down the traditional barrier between the professor and students. According to his good friend, Eberhard Bethge, it was at this time that Bonhoeffer became much more active in the life of the church. Bethge has reported that "the young theologian engaged himself in a disciplined church life which was quite unfamiliar to his family and theological teachers."[5]

During this period Bonhoeffer, the Christian, also turned his attention toward the menace of Nazism which was permeating Germany. In 1933 Hitler had gained control of Germany, and the universities and churches offered little resistance to this new form of tyranny. Bonhoeffer believed that the Third Reich, the new thousand years of Aryan domination of the world, was an enemy of Jesus Christ and all that the gospel stood for. Hitler preached hatred, while the message of Christ was love and reconciliation. Bonhoeffer decided to challenge what he called the great masquerade of evil. With the Nazis, evil had disguised itself as goodness and light; it presented itself in the guise of a better tomorrow for Germany. Bonhoeffer wrote, "The great masquerade of evil has played havoc with all our ethical concepts."[6] He realized that appeals to conscience were of no value when dealing with Hitler. He understood that the use of reason was of no consequence for the political philosophy of Nazism. Bonhoeffer claimed that Hitler must be opposed from the very center of the Christian faith. Followers of Christ must stand and be counted in their opposition to Nazi violence and terror. Bonhoeffer understood what Christians have always understood but not always acted upon, namely, that whenever anyone is victimized by another individual or group, then Jesus Christ himself is victimized. The non-Aryan laws of 1933 compelled Bonhoeffer to speak out publicly against Hitler in the name of Christ. These racist laws led to the definition of Jews as nonpersons in Germany. Bonhoeffer understood the deadly implications of these laws. He called the churches of Germany to action against the Third Reich:

> . . . when the Church sees the state exercising too little or too much law and order, it is its task not simply to bind the wounds of the victims beneath the wheel, but also to put a spoke in the wheel itself.[7]

Bonhoeffer was determined to help "put a spoke in the wheel" of Nazi power. In the years preceding the Second World War, he worked against Hitler's policies from within the German church. This led to a ban on Bonhoeffer's teaching and publishing in Germany. He was harassed by the gestapo, and was arrested but not held by the Nazis in 1937. After the outbreak of war in 1939, Bonhoeffer joined in a conspiracy to assassinate Hitler. He had determined that he had no other responsible course of action remaining. The spoke must be placed in the

wheel before Germany destroyed herself along with her enemies.

When the attempt on Hitler's life failed in July of 1944, Bonhoeffer had already been imprisoned as an enemy of the state.
It was not long before Bonhoeffer was linked to the conspiracy,
and on April 9, 1945, he was hanged by the gestapo. An English
officer who had been a fellow prisoner with Bonhoeffer said of
him, "He was one of the very few persons I have met for whom
God was real and always near. . . . "[8] Eberhard Bethge has
conveyed this description to us of Bonhoeffer's last hours:

> In the grey dawn of that Monday, April 9, there took place at
> Flossenbürg the execution of those who were not in any circum-
> stances to survive. The camp doctor saw Bonhoeffer kneeling in
> the preparation cell and praying fervently.[9]

Bonhoeffer died a lonely death. His parents and his fiancee did
not learn of his fate until many months after the war's end.

This is certainly a dramatic story, and it is all the more dramatic
for Christians because Bonhoeffer's life was motivated by one
unrelenting question, who is Jesus Christ for us today? We shall
discover that from the time Bonhoeffer became a Christian until
his death, he would not let go of this question. He believed that
his future and the future of Christianity depended upon how
we answer that question.

The Person of Jesus Christ

After becoming Christian we are drawn to the question of
who Jesus Christ is in a new way. We ask the question with a
great deal more intensity. It is now a personal matter. This
dynamic process can also be found in Bonhoeffer's life. In the
decade before his imprisonment and subsequent death, he moved
closer and closer to a personal encounter with his Christ. His
1933 lectures on Christology (Doctrine of Jesus Christ) at the
University of Berlin were a significant point of departure for
Bonhoeffer. Here we can observe how this new Christian's
thought became Christ-centered.

At the beginning of his lectures Bonhoeffer informed his students that he would depart from the standard academic ap-
proaches to the study of Jesus Christ. Rather than begin with

the historical questions, he planned to start with a contemporary question. Is there evidence of the existence of Jesus Christ in the world today? He answered yes. The church is a fellowship of the living Christ. Earlier in his doctoral dissertation Bonhoeffer had described the church as "Christ existing as community."[10] Now he clarified his assertion with the traditional insights of his own Lutheran tradition. Christ was present in the preaching of God's Word; he was present in the administration of the sacraments; and he was present in the fellowship of the community.

He added to this, however, a new emphasis. Perhaps it is better to say that he reemphasized an ancient Christian truth. Christ is present in the life of the individual believer or he is not present at all. Bonhoeffer insisted that the living Christ cannot exist as some kind of isolated principle or eternal law. Christ must exist in a personal way "for me." Here the young German theologian drew upon the wisdom of Martin Luther and the apostle Paul himself. Jesus Christ can be known only in relationship. He is the one to be encountered; we are to live in Christ, and Christ is to live in us. Even in the lecture hall Bonhoeffer was prepared to argue that Jesus Christ has no true meaning unless we are willing to be grasped by his personal reality. He put it this way: ". . . Christ can never be thought of in his being in himself, but only in his relationship to me."[11]

Bonhoeffer informed his students that the question of Jesus Christ must always be the personal "who." This is evident from the New Testament itself. When Jesus raised the question of his identity for others, he asked, "Who do men say that I am?" (Mark 8:27). According to Bonhoeffer, it is easy to get sidetracked from this question. The early church, for example, took up the philosophical question of Jesus' two natures (the human and the divine). How was God in Christ? As interesting as the questions of Christ's double nature might be, they can easily lead us away from a personal encounter. Likewise, the modern church is dangerously close to becoming lost in the equally intriguing question of "what?" What does it mean to say that God revealed God's self in Jesus Christ? Once again these are interesting questions, but they divert us from the primary question, "who" is Jesus Christ?

Bonhoeffer forced his students to face this question squarely and without qualification. It is a matter for us as well. Like Bonhoeffer, we need to recognize that there is a certain "givenness" to the Christian faith. That God was in Jesus Christ reconciling the world is our starting point. We can ask many questions which seek to probe behind that affirmation, but in the end we accept its truth in faith. It is at this level that the question of "who" becomes real. Who is this that is redeemer of the world? Who is this that we are asked to follow? Who is it that calls us forth and demands so very much of us? These were the real questions of Christology for Bonhoeffer.

It is this person, Jesus Christ, who has led us into a new relationship. Jesus Christ is a new reality to which we relate. In this sense he is more than a good teacher, or another prophet, or a wise sage. Christ not only teaches the truth, but for the follower he is the truth. Jesus Christ and truth are one and the same. Bonhoeffer asked his students a question in relation to this proposition. It is also a question for us.

> But what happens if someone appears with the claim that he . . . not only *has* a word but *is* the Word? Here our being is invaded by a new being. Here the highest authority in the world so far, the prophet, is at an end. This is no longer a holy man, a reformer, a prophet, but the Son. The question is no longer, "What or whence are you?" The question here concerns revelation itself.[12]

Can we relate to this sort of revelation in a personal way? One thing is certain for Bonhoeffer. Should the revelation of God in Jesus Christ touch our lives in a personal encounter, then we will be compelled to follow.

Disciples of Jesus Christ

It is not enough simply to talk about Jesus Christ. Bonhoeffer knew that he had to follow Christ as well as lecture about him in the classroom. Faithful action was a necessary corollary of faith itself. In fact Bonhoeffer claimed that we Christians have gotten the order between action and faith confused. Some would argue that we must believe before we can act. This is by and

large the accepted order of things. However, Bonhoeffer claimed
it was exactly the opposite. We must act in order to really believe.
His thinking is derived from the stories of Jesus and his original
disciples. He noted that Jesus did not ask his disciples initially
to offer a confession of faith in him. He simply met them by the
lakeside, or in the marketplace, and said, "Follow me."

In his book on the Christian faith, *The Cost of Discipleship*,
Bonhoeffer stressed the primacy of action in the Christian life.
Referring to the twelve apostles, he wrote: "The response of the
disciples is an act of obedience, not a confession of faith in
Jesus."[13] That confession came later. The church has always had
a tough time remembering the importance of action. We all know
how much easier it is to speak than it is to act. This is equally
true in the case of our commitment to Jesus Christ. But Bonhoeffer declared in his day that the time for words had ended
and the time for action had come.

According to Bonhoeffer, Christians in Germany had lost sense
of the meaning of serving Jesus Christ. Most had stood by
silently as Hitler unleashed his reign of terror. The irony of Nazi
Germany was that many Christians were willing to confess Jesus
Christ as Lord, but very few were prepared to follow him in the
ways which made for righteousness (justice). The church, said
Bonhoeffer, was living off a "cheap grace." He defined this grace
as a good which was sold in the marketplace to the lowest
bidder.[14] The church had sacrificed the integrity of Jesus Christ
and his cause, for the price of popularity and privilege.

The church was preaching forgiveness without repentance. It
presented baptism without instruction; it offered communion
without confession; and it taught grace without discipleship. In
other words, Christians were telling themselves that everything
would be okay if only they believed. God would take care of
Hitler in due time. However, the corollary of action was missing.
As Christians confessed, millions of innocent people died. Where
was the Christian witness of action which was to accompany
the witness of word?

We must always be careful as the church of Jesus Christ that
we not become more concerned with our own survival than with
the work of Jesus Christ. Bonhoeffer reminded the church that

it must be prepared to pay the cost of discipleship. Only in this way could Christians remain faithful to Christ. Grace is not cheap; it is indeed very costly. The love of God in Jesus Christ is like the biblical pearl of great price or the treasure hidden in the field. When found, it means everything. Bonhoeffer said that now was the time for "costly grace" in the churches of Germany. We must be willing to give our all.

> Such grace is *costly* because it calls us to follow, and it is *grace* because it calls us to follow *Jesus Christ*. It is costly because it costs man his life, and it is grace because it gives man the only true life. It is costly because it condemns sin, and grace because it justifies the sinner. Above all, it is *costly* because it cost God the life of his Son. . . .[15]

The call to follow Jesus Christ in any age is the call to discipleship. In his own times, Bonhoeffer was adamant about the need for Christians to be faithful to Christ in their actions. He declared: "Cheap grace is the deadly enemy of our Church. We are fighting to-day for costly grace."[16]

In a move to overcome the "cheap grace" of his church, Bonhoeffer joined with a minority of German Christians in the formation of the Confessing Church. This church was an illegal synod set up within German Protestantism to combat the Nazi-controlled Evangelical church in Germany. Martin Niemoeller and others, including Bonhoeffer, gave leadership to this underground church. In the Barmen Declaration of 1934, the new church declared that its only head could be Jesus Christ, and Hitler had no authority over this church.

Solidarity in Jesus Christ

Christians find strength in one another. Bonhoeffer appreciated the truth of this statement; thus in 1935 when he was asked to direct the seminary of the Confessing Church, he sought to build a Christian community. Under his guidance the young seminarians of the Confessing Church shared together in a common life of study and prayer, work and play. Since they continually lived under the threat of being discovered and disbanded, they valued deeply the time they had together. Bonhoeffer hoped to create a fellowship within this illegal seminary which would sustain these men in the struggles which were before them. He worked hard to identify the power of Christ's spirit in their midst.

Bonhoeffer taught his seminarians that their sole reason for being together was Jesus Christ. They had been called together in his name. The life which they had to share had its primary reality in that "fact." Christian community needed to be built upon the cornerstone of Christ. Gathering together and defining the fellowship according to individual experiences would never do; experiences vary. The only solid ground on which to establish Christian community was Christ. We may find this statement to be self-evident or we may find it to be overly simplistic; in any case, Bonhoeffer argued that the recognition of Christ at the heart of fellowship is absolutely critical for Christian living.

He wrote about finding Christ in the center of Christian fellowship in his book about this seminary experience called *Life Together*.

Christianity means community through Jesus Christ and in Jesus Christ. No Christian community is more or less than this. Whether it be a brief, single encounter or the daily fellowship of years, Christian community is only this. We belong to one another only through and in Jesus Christ.[17]

In order to stand against the Nazis, the Christian would need to draw upon support from the community which lived through and in Jesus Christ. This strong sense of community support was lacking in the German church. Our churches may not be far from this predicament. It seems that Christianity is always in danger of losing its community life in Christ. Perhaps our individualism keeps us from recognizing Jesus Christ in any kind of corporate sense. But Bonhoeffer insisted upon this important dimension of the living Christ and he celebrated "Christ existing as community."

Our resistance, indeed the church's resistance, to finding Christ in community may also be due to our refusal to do the hard work of community building. We discover so many ways to avoid the demands of fellowship. We claim we cannot participate in community because it compromises our individuality. The community will not allow for enough self-expression. This protest, however, is often simply an evasion of Christ himself. Does not Christ call us to surrender ourselves to him? Might this not be true for his community as well?

Another kind of resistance to community in Christ is our excuse that we have nothing to offer the fellowship. Yet Christ accepts us as we are; would not his community do the same? We are called to bring ourselves as gifts to the community. Christ will not reject us. Bonhoeffer noted that these and other forms of resistance to fellowship are dangerous obstacles to a life shared together in Christ. The building of Christian community is indeed hard work.

The young theologian had many words of caution for the seminarians as they sought to establish a Christian fellowship. His greatest concern was focused upon the dynamics of a Christian life lived in community. Maturity was stressed. He cautioned: *"Let him who cannot be alone beware of community"* and *"Let him who is not in community beware of being alone."*[18] We are not to flee from ourselves into community, nor are we to take comfort in community to the extent that we completely lose ourselves. In Christian living, the self and the common life are to be celebrated together. Christ is fully present in the affirmation of both. Christ is not real for us without the personal encounter, but it is also true that he is not alive without fellowship. Christ's reality embraces both the individual life of the Christian and the life of the Christian in community with others. This was an invaluable lesson for Bonhoeffer and his seminarians as they faced the Nazi menace. It is also an important lesson for us today.

Christ as Our Contemporary

Nothing is more real to the Christian than the living Christ. Bonhoeffer was beginning to discover this truth in his own life, but it did not completely fill his consciousness until the time of his imprisonment. For the first time in his life he truly came to understand what it meant to view life from the perspective of Christ. He was now among the world's disinherited; he was among the people whom Jesus called "the blessed ones" (Matthew 5-6). If Jesus Christ were to be fully present and contemporary for Bonhoeffer, he now realized that he would need to view life "from below."

Viewing life from a lofty position of power and privilege had led the German nation to the greatest distortions of truth. The church in Germany also preferred this vantage point. National pride resulted in a spiritual imperialism. The church thought it could do no wrong. Its other worldly spirituality had served only to validate the tyranny of Hitler. Another viewpoint was called for. Bonhoeffer declared:

> We have for once learnt to see the great events of history from below, from the perspective of the outcast, the suspects, the maltreated, the powerless, the oppressed, the reviled—in short, from the perspective of those who suffer. . . . We have to learn that personal suffering is a more effective key, a more rewarding principle for exploring the world in thought and action than personal good fortune.[19]

Bonhoeffer was now prepared to learn more about Christ and Christ's world as he entered into the suffering of Christ. He could presently share life more fully with Christ because he identified more fully with the suffering of others.

According to Bonhoeffer, Jesus Christ had become "the man for others." In the form of a servant, Christ continued to minister to a world filled with pain. This was the Christ "who, though he was in the form of God, did not count equality with God a thing to be grasped, but emptied himself, taking the form of a servant, being born in the likeness of men" (Philippians 2:6). Jesus Christ brought transcendence into the midst of life through his own suffering. In this sense, God's kingdom is not a realm off in another world; it is completely present in the human-divine experience of Christ in this world.

In the kind of world in which he lived, Bonhoeffer believed it was not enough simply to say that God cares. Somehow that had a very hollow sound to it. What needed to be said was that this God who cares in Jesus Christ also suffers with us in Jesus Christ. Only a suffering God can make a difference. This notion is a radical inversion of traditional ways of viewing God. This God is not detached and far off. This God is close at hand and is also very vulnerable to the world's suffering. Bonhoeffer put it this way:

God let himself be pushed out of the world on to the cross. He is weak and powerless in the world, and that is precisely the way, the only way, in which he is with us and helps us. Matthew 8:17 makes it quite clear that Christ helps us, not by virtue of his omnipotence, but by virtue of his weakness and suffering.
. . . . The Bible directs man to God's powerlessness and suffering; only the suffering God can help.[20]

Jesus, therefore, comes to us in weakness and powerlessness. These qualities, not given positive value in our world, become the basis of our redemption in Jesus Christ. Jesus is like the prisoner and the outcast; he is the victim, and by the world's standards he is impotent and without power. But since he is the Son of God, he brings transcendence and transformation to our earthly life. In Jesus Christ we once again discover God— not the God who is an omnipotent king, but the God who has truly come face-to-face with the world's pain and bears it as a parent for a child.

In his last years Bonhoeffer did a great deal of thinking about the God who is re-presented to us in Jesus Christ. He observed from his prison cell that many people did not find God to be a meaningful reality in their lives. The world had become very secular (nonreligious) in its outlook. However, Bonhoeffer was not necessarily disturbed by this development. He viewed it as a logical outcome of a world which was "coming of age." He was not referring to a moral "coming of age," but rather to the development of a new consciousness. It was a simple fact that most people no longer explained life using God as a "working hypothesis."[21] Science could explain life without God, and the general public merely held on to religion as it held on to superstition.

Bonhoeffer was convinced that the Christian faith needed to shed its old religious skin if it were to survive after the war. Christianity needed to hold to Jesus Christ, but many of the religious trappings could and should be discarded. At one point Bonhoeffer wrote from prison that Christianity in the future would be a very simple affair. In addition to being Christ-centered, its basic marks would involve two things: prayer and righteous (just) action.[22]

Jesus Christ as "the man for others" would form the basis of

Bonhoeffer's nonreligious interpretation of Christianity. This is
not the reduction of Christianity to a mere ethical level as some
have thought in reading Bonhoeffer. It is rather an insistence
upon making Christ the true center of Christian life and faith.
The ethical dimension is strong; we are called to follow Christ
as "the man for others." We are to imitate his passion for the
oppressed. But transcendence is also present. What we are dealing with is none other than the living God present in our midst.
This is a God who is present in the middle of life, and not only
on the unknown boundaries of life and death. In Bonhoeffer's
words we encounter:

> God in human form—not, as in oriental religions, in animal form,
> monstrous, chaotic, remote, and terrifying, nor in the conceptual
> forms of the absolute, metaphysical, infinite, etc., nor yet in the
> Greek divine-human form of "man in himself," but "the man for
> others," and therefore the Crucified, the man who lives out the
> transcendent.[23]

With these words the prisoner Bonhoeffer, not certain of his
own future, nevertheless set the clear future for Christian living.
We are to return to Christ, but not as if we are making a pilgrimage to a shrine. We are to return to the living Christ who
is present for us in our devotion and discipleship. Christ is our
contemporary.

Who Is Jesus Christ Today?

With the help of Dietrich Bonhoeffer, we have been able to
learn several things about Christ's meaning for us. First of all,
it makes a great deal of difference how we ask our questions
about Jesus Christ. Should we ask out of a casual curiosity, we
will probably not get very far. But as in the case with Bonhoeffer,
should we find ourselves suddenly grasped by the question of
faith, we could be facing a much deeper set of questions. We
may very well be drawn to ask the personal question out of our
own lives, Who is this Jesus Christ? Only when we find ourselves in this predicament of questioning faith does the question
of Jesus Christ become a live issue for us.

In the second place, the question of Jesus Christ, if it is asked
in all seriousness, leads to the question of discipleship. Bon-

hoeffer has demonstrated to us the importance of action in the Christian life. The question of Jesus Christ does indeed challenge us to consider the cost of discipleship. We have not answered the question of who Jesus Christ is for us today until we are ready to live out the answer in faithful obedience. This is the crossroad to which every follower of Jesus Christ comes. We must decide which way to go, the way of the disciple or the way of the apostate.

A third factor involved in the question of Jesus Christ is the question of the meaning of Christian fellowship. We cannot ask who Jesus Christ is today without in the same breath asking where he is to be found. Bonhoeffer indicated that the living Christ was to be experienced in Christian community. Life in fellowship with other followers of Christ can be a genuine source of strength and encouragement. But beyond even this, life in the fellowship of other Christians can introduce us to Jesus Christ himself. Life in the Spirit of Christ with others brings us into contact with the Holy Spirit. Christ's presence exists in its fullest expression in a life shared with others in his name.

Finally, the question of Jesus Christ joins us with our contemporary world. In the final analysis, Bonhoeffer taught us that Christ does not belong simply to the individual follower. He does not even belong in any exclusive sense to his church. Jesus Christ belongs to the world, and it is in the world that he can be found in his fullest expression. Those who seek to know Jesus Christ today must be prepared to walk with his Spirit along the path of those who suffer in our world. Jesus Christ stands with those who are oppressed and denied their humanity. He is truly "the man for others." As his followers, we too must be for others. Bonhoeffer has helped us understand that to know Christ is to develop a new consciousness, and it is this consciousness which helps us view life from the vantage point of the least among us.

Who, then, is Jesus Christ for us today? As was indicated at the beginning of this chapter, the final answer to this question must ultimately be our own. Like Bonhoeffer, our answer will come to us within the time and place of our own lives. And like Bonhoeffer, we too may discover that "Christ died for the world, and it is only in the midst of the world that Christ is Christ."²⁴

Recommended Reading

Dietrich Bonhoeffer
The Cost of Discipleship. New York: The Macmillan Company, 1963.
Life Together. New York: Harper & Row, Publishers, Inc., 1954.
Letters and Papers from Prison. New York: The Macmillan Company, 1972.
Ethics. New York: The Macmillan Company, 1965.

Books about Dietrich Bonhoeffer
Eberhard Bethge, *Dietrich Bonhoeffer.* New York: Harper & Row, Publishers, Inc., 1970.
Eberhard Bethge, *Costly Grace.* New York: Harper & Row, Publishers, Inc., 1979.
A. J. Klassen, ed. *A Bonhoeffer Legacy.* Grand Rapids, Michigan: Eerdmans, 1981.

NOTES

¹Dietrich Bonhoeffer, *Letters and Papers from Prison*, Enlarged ed. (New York: The Macmillan Company, 1972; London: SCM Press, Ltd., 1953, 1967, 1971), p. 279.
²Dietrich Bonhoeffer, *No Rusty Swords* (New York: Harper & Row, Publishers, Inc., 1965), p. 78.
³Eberhard Bethge, *Costly Grace* (New York: Harper & Row, Publishers, Inc., 1979), p. 29.
⁴Peter Vorking, ed. *Bonhoeffer in a World Come of Age* (Philadelphia: Fortress Press, 1968), p. 80.
⁵*Ibid.*, p. 79.
⁶Bonhoeffer, *Letters and Papers from Prison*, p. 4.
⁷Quoted in Bethge, *Costly Grace*, p. 62.
⁸Dietrich Bonhoeffer, *Life Together* (New York: Harper & Row, Publishers, Inc., 1954), p. 21.
⁹Dietrich Bonhoeffer, *Letters and Papers from Prison*, 3rd. rev. ed. (London: SCM Press, 1967), pp. 232ff., quoted in Heinrich Ott, *Reality and Faith* (Philadelphia: Fortress Press, 1972), p. 257.
¹⁰Bethge, *Costly Grace*, p. 149.
¹¹Dietrich Bonhoeffer, *Christ the Center* (New York: Harper & Row, Publishers, Inc., 1960), p. 47.
¹²*Ibid.*, p. 37.
¹³Dietrich Bonhoeffer, *The Cost of Discipleship* (New York: The Macmillan Company, 1963; London: SCM Press, Ltd., 1959), p. 61.
¹⁴*Ibid.*, p. 45.
¹⁵*Ibid.*, pp. 47-48.

[16] *Ibid.*, p. 45.
[17] Bonhoeffer, *Life Together*, p. 21.
[18] *Ibid.*, p. 77.
[19] Bonhoeffer, *Letters and Papers from Prison*, (Macmillan edition), p. 17.
[20] *Ibid.*, pp. 360-361.
[21] *Ibid.*, p. 325.
[22] *Ibid.*, p. 300.
[23] *Ibid.*, pp. 381-382.
[24] Dietrich Bonhoeffer, *Ethics* (New York: The Macmillan Company, 1955; London: SCM Press, Ltd., 1955), p. 206 (in paperback edition, 1965).

2

CARLYLE MARNEY:
What Does It Mean to Be Fully Human?

When I look at thy heavens, the work
   of thy fingers,
the moon and the stars which thou hast
   established;
what is man that thou art mindful of
   him,
and the son of man that thou dost care
   for him?

Yet thou has made him little less
   than God,
and dost crown him with glory and honor.

—Psalm 8:3-5

What does it mean to be fully human? This is obviously a question which reaches beyond the scope of conventional reason and definition. The question implies that we have not yet reached our completion as human beings. Perhaps there is more to life than we now recognize? The psalmist had this in mind when he pondered the meaning of life in relation to the universe and its Creator. Like the psalmist, we too want to know where we fit into the grand design of the cosmos. Can we find personal meaning in a world which itself seems so vast and impersonal? Who are we as human beings? What role do we play in the larger scheme of things?

These are indeed important questions for us, but they are questions which are in danger of being lost in our computerized age. Today our main concern is to get somewhere faster, to make things bigger, and to accumulate all that we can. In our frenzied, technological world, there exists little room for the question of personal meaning. We are numbers, statistics, and figures on graphs and charts. We have lost the psalmist's question. Yet even in our swirling, topsy-turvy, materialistic world, there are a few who persist in asking the question which is so disarming because of its simplicity—who are we as human beings and what does it mean to be fully human? What is the nature and destiny of our species? Do we, in fact, have any real connection to our universe? Can we find any kind of relationship between the Creator and ourselves?

A master of these kinds of questions was the pastor-theologian Carlyle Marney. This Southern Baptist preacher liked to say that each of us has one basic question in life. We may ask the question in many different forms, but when it comes right down to it we each have a singular concern. Marney's question was clearly articulated in his preaching and writing. He was concerned with nothing other than the meaning of our humanity. He often phrased his question in the most direct language: "What does it mean to be human?"[1] Behind this question was a lifelong search to discover humanity in its fullest expression. With Marney there is a sense that God is not finished with us yet. The human race is not complete in its nature, not yet mature.

As a pilgrim along the way to a fuller humanity, Marney is an exciting traveling companion. Should we chart his course, we will find a most challenging path. Our guide on this journey is unconventional and even abrasive at times, but he is worth following because the trail he blazes brings us back to ourselves. As we shall discover, Marney is relentless in his pursuit of the meaning of the human equation. He asks the right questions; he seeks the balance which will bring wholeness and completeness to our lives. We would do well to retrace this man's steps in order that we too might gain a clearer vision of humanity in its fullness and maturity.

Charting His Own Course

Carlyle Marney (1916-1978) was a Renaissance man in Baptist garb; he was an enigma to some and an inspiration to many.

Among Southern Baptist preachers he was the only one of his generation to gain ecumenical stature in American religious life. He identified with the Christian gospel of his Tennessee mountain roots and he embraced many of the cultural and intellectual trends of the modern world. He was equally at home with Baptists, Methodists, Lutherans, Episcopalians, Catholics, and secularists of all varieties. He despised labels and insisted that his own tribal designation of "Baptist" was merely an adjective. The noun for Marney was "Christian," but even this was sometimes insufficient, for his quest was universal. He claimed that he would follow light wherever it led him, once he determined it to be light.

In Marney's case, his light came from two distinct historical sources: the world of classical learning (humanism) and the world of biblical revelation (Christianity). He wrote, "I propose two very old answers in combination—two very old roadbeds run together at last—to project a possible access road to a better and higher way for now."[2] It was Marney's belief that classical learning and biblical religion both spoke of humanity's high calling. Some Christians preferred to drive a wedge between humanism and traditional Christian belief. This was wrong in Marney's estimate. Both had much to offer when it came to the question of who we are as human beings. Marney made it clear that he was an unabashed advocate of Christian humanism. He liked to confess, "Humanism has always been my heresy."[3]

Today, as we know, many Christians are still uncomfortable with anything that smacks of humanism. Some Christians find the humanist's emphasis upon human growth and development to be godless in intent and contrary to the spirit of the gospel. For some traditionalists the humanist emphasis upon human achievement detracts from God's glory. It is as if God is being edged out of the picture. Marney disagrees. He concedes that some humanists have abandoned God, but he argues that is not the case for thousands of humanists who continue to express their Christian faith as well as their commitment to humanistic values.

Marney was willing to risk the "heresy" of humanism because of the humanist's effort to preserve human value. He was very

much aware of a history of Christian theology in which the
human race was declared totally depraved so that God's goodness could remain pure and undefiled. Marney would have none
of that. Some theologians had made sin the major doctrine of
the Christian faith. But Marney viewed this as unbiblical in
nature. The central doctrine of faith was God's grace and the
forgiving love which attended it. Marney would not permit the
theologians of sin to rule the day. He valued human life and
would not demote it to the depths of depravity to which it was
assigned by many theologians.

As we shall see, Marney chose to emphasize the biblical concept that the human race is a creation in God's image. This view
resulted in a positive picture of humanity. Certainly we are
flawed by sin, but the image of God in which we were created
is not completely tarnished. Marney sensed that human life is
filled with God-given potential and unlike many of his contemporaries in the South, he did not dwell upon the sinfulness and
weakness of the human race. Marney wanted to place the theological emphasis on another "syllable"—it was time to recognize
that the human race was blessed as well as cursed.

In the cultural surroundings in which Marney was raised, the
"old-time religion" of Protestant fundamentalism was domi-
nant. Born to a good Baptist family in Harrison, Tennessee, in
1916, he was cautioned by friends to avoid the pitfalls of mod-
ernism. He heard in his youth about the Scopes Monkey Trial
which was taking place in nearby Cleveland, Tennessee. Godless
proponents of Darwin's theory of evolution were trying to teach
a view of creation without the Creator. Men like Clarence Darrow
were making "monkeys" out of God-fearing Americans like
William Jennings Bryan. At all costs, young Marney was cautioned to stay clear of atheistic science and modernist religion.

Marney, however, was a maverick spirit. He ignored all advice
and became the worst of all possible things: a liberal-minded
preacher. His natural proclivity was to bolt at any advice which
was given in an authoritarian manner. And there was a tremendous amount of this type of advice available in Marney's
Southern Baptist setting. The Southern Baptist Convention did
not quite know what to do with him. Some felt he was over-

educated and had lost his faith; he had earned an advanced degree in theology from Southern Baptist Seminary in Louisville. He himself never felt comfortable with denominational structures or the piety which accompanied them; so he charted his own course.

In addition to his rebellious personality, Marney also had a magnificent sense of humor. He was leery of people who took themselves too seriously and he often delighted in making himself the brunt of a good joke. He understood that the establishment of our genuine humanity required that we have the ability to laugh at ourselves. Many "Marney stories" have circulated through his congregations and among his friends. One of the most revealing may be the anecdote told by Nancy Geer, a member of the Myers Park Baptist Church in Charlotte, North Carolina, where Marney pastored from 1958 to 1967. Geer's four-year-old daughter had been hospitalized, and Marney, who loved children, paid a visit to this little parishioner in her hospital room. Geer was not present when Marney visited her daughter. Later when she found out about the visit, she asked her daughter if she had recognized the man who had visited her. Without hesitation, the small patient replied, "Yes, he is our creature." Marney loved to tell that story on himself, for he realized that in so many ways he was a strange "creature," as well as a preacher, to many in his congregations.[4]

The Human Side of Preaching

Marney struck a very impressive figure from the pulpit. With his tremendous bass voice and his extraordinary grasp of the English language, he could overwhelm his congregations. Many have reported that he appeared bigger than life—the power of his ideas and the deep tones of his voice caused one fellow clergyman to wonder if that combination might not be how God sounded.[5] Preaching for Marney was indeed a great event, and he knew how to get to where the people lived. Stuart Dickson, another member of the Myers Park church, has reported this remembrance of Marney's preaching.

> I remember his first sermon. I had never seen him before, but I remember his stepping into the pulpit. . . . His hair was still red

and he was a completely and totally unexpected, different type of preacher. As I remember, his first sermon was, "Here I am and let me tell you a little bit about where I think we can be and go." You knew you were in the presence of someone who had an extra gift.[6]

There was, however, another side to Marney the preacher. It was a very human side; he was often plagued by doubts and fears as an interpreter of God's Word. "I am stricken dumb, between Sundays, at my own audacity," wrote Marney.[7] He marveled at how he could speak so convincingly about God from the pulpit, and yet have so many questions about his own personal encounter with God. This kind of openness and honesty scared away some of his parishioners, but many more were attracted by his candor.

This human side of Marney's preaching carried over into the other areas of his pastoral work. His own sense of vulnerability as a human being made him a sensitive counselor of others. One friend of Marney has said, "I don't think he even knew how to say 'no' or how to sort out his priorities for himself or for meeting the needs of other people . . . I never saw him when he wasn't serious about somebody's hurting."[8] Marney cared so much for others that he would risk direct confrontation in order to cause people to deal with feelings they had suppressed, feelings which prevented growth as long as they remained buried.

On one occasion in a group-counseling situation, Marney interrupted a minister who had been talking at great length in glowing terms about his father. Marney directly addressed the surprised pastor, "Your father was a 'bastard,' wasn't he, and he was probably very hard to get along with, wasn't he?" This confrontation threw the minister into a rage, but soon he began to deal with the negative, suppressed feelings about his father which he had kept bottled up for so long. As a result, healing was able to take place. Marney knew that sometimes a festering wound must be lanced before health can be restored.[9]

In this regard, Marney was an agitator of the first order. He loved to challenge people's sacred cows. He wrote, "I like to make people angry because that's the way you find out who the person really is."[10] He would confront people with their own prejudices, and he loved to back people into corners. In this way he sought to get at the real issues in people's lives. The masks had to be removed. Marney made people deal with their real selves, for better or for worse.

In addition to his confrontational manner, there was also the affirmative side of Marney. His familiar question to his friends, "How is it with you?" was an open invitation to share life together. And Marney always seemed to have the right words to say for the sake of encouragement. A colleague, Charles Milford, said this about his friend and associate in ministry: "Marney turned me loose. Marney freed me to go where I wanted to go, where I wanted to be. It was in that sense that he had his greatest influence."[11]

The power to unbind and set free was a gift Marney revealed to me in our only meeting shortly before his death in 1978. As a college chaplain living in Oregon, I had serious questions about whether I was in the right place for my ministry. I was uncertain as to my calling, and I wondered to myself about my future in the work I was doing. Although I said nothing directly to Marney about my situation, he sensed that I needed to be set free to perform my ministry—I was bound by my own private questions and I longed for a word which would liberate me. He took me aside during a dinner meeting and looked me straight in the eye. "If I were a young man in the 1970s," he said, "you know where I would go?" I did not respond. He continued, "I would go to the Pacific Northwest—there is real excitement here, a real frontier!" That was all I needed to hear. Marney had given me permission to do what I really wanted to do all along—to continue my life as a college chaplain in Oregon. His affirmation had given me permission to be myself, something I could not release myself to be.[12]

Finding Our Humanity in the Image of God

At the very center of Marney's affirmation of life, we find the biblical notion of our creation in God's image. In his preaching and his writing he constantly returned to this theme of our creation in the image of God (*imago dei*). For him the most important of all discoveries for biblical people was their awareness of their close proximity to the Creator. In Genesis 1:27 we read, "So God created man in his own image . . . male and female he created them." This, in Marney's eyes, was a recognition of a reality he called "the great Hebrew discovery." In his words, "The great Hebrew discovery was that God who is One has put his image in us all."[13]

Since we are all created in the *imago dei*, this places a very high premium on our worth as human beings. It suggests that we are creatures to be greatly valued. Being fully human, then, must have something to do with God's image—but what? Marney did not choose to develop the idea of our creation in God's image in the traditional ways of most Christian teaching. Many theologians had taken this Genesis passage to mean that we human beings have some divine spark within us that cannot be extinguished. This divine spark was viewed as an evidence of our soul's immortality.

Marney's interpretation of the *imago dei* went in the opposite direction. God's image was a biblical theme intended to speak to us of our present humanity rather than our possible divinity. Creation in the image of God meant that we were indeed created with wisdom, creativity, imagination, compassion, and many of the other attributes we normally associate with the Creator. This does make us much "like" the God of the universe, but it does not make us God. Quite the reverse is true. Creation in the *imago dei* is a celebration of our humanity, albeit a humanity lived close to God.

The distinction between the Creator and the created order, including we human beings, is an ironclad separation in the Bible. Things are in their proper relationship whenever the differences between Creator and creature are not forgotten. The moment human beings (Adam and Eve) sought to be something they could not be, namely divine, the whole cosmos was thrown out of balance, and sin entered the world. Viewing our creation in God's image as an indication of our own latent divinity only helps to accentuate an unhealthy desire to become godlike rather than fully human.

According to Marney, we humans have always been uncomfortable in our own skins. Indeed, the real sin for Adam and

Eve was their unwillingness to accept their rightful place in God's creation. Adam and Eve wanted to be more—they preferred to be God and to have the Creator's knowledge of good and evil. In this regard, people have always desired more, denying their humanity and longing to be among the gods. As Marney has said, "The Garden of Eden is not primal—it is formal—universal—everywhere repeated."[14]

In Marney's estimate, our ability to affirm our humanity as God's gift to us in creation has been thwarted by our own ambiguous feelings about being human. We know we are *homoanthropos*: we stand upright, the only two-legged creatures to sustain a vertical posture. But at middle age we begin to bend again. We are aware of our success as *homo-faber*; we make instruments and build civilizations. But we have also mastered our skills at building massive weapons of destruction. We are *homo-sapiens*; we can think, acquire knowledge, and solve complex problems. Unfortunately, our genius has helped to create even larger problems whose dimensions threaten the very existence of our planet Earth.[15]

Life's ambiguities are further complicated by the fact that we are the only creatures who know that we are going to die. We cannot seem to shake off an acute sense of our own finitude. Perhaps this is why we want to be gods—gods do not die! Marney has noted that we are constantly looking for something beyond ourselves, something that has more permanency than we do. In this sense, we are *homo-religiosus*; we are religious creatures searching for some lasting connection between ourselves and our universe.

However, raising the religious question as human beings does not necessarily bring comfortable solutions. In many cases our anxiety about being human is increased by our spiritual awareness. The solutions are often not forthcoming. Many of us feel even more adrift once the possibility of meaning is raised. But there is hope in Marney's purview of the human race. It comes from a theological assertion; namely, that God is not finished with creation. In Marney's opinion, God continues to work within creation—God continues to pursue the human race. This ongoing creative effort of God can be detected in much of nature and history, but it has its clearest expression in Jesus of Nazareth.

Finding Our Humanity in Jesus Christ

Marney was fond of saying that Jesus of Nazareth was the human race's great "unexploited advantage." Looking at Jesus, he reported, "We really know what man is like—full-grown."[16] Here was the way out of confusion for humankind. Indeed, here was the way back to God's original creative intent. Marney believed that the complete meaning of our creation in God's image came to fruition not in "original" creation, but in the new creation, Jesus Christ. This was perhaps Marney's greatest theological contribution to the discussion of the question of who we are as human beings.

Jesus, in Marney's estimate, embodied (or incarnated) in human life what had always been true, but mostly forgotten: that is, that God's intent for us is to become fully human and not fully divine. In Jesus Christ we can discover once again our full humanity. With Christ we are set free to become true sons and daughters of God; in other words, we can become completed (whole) human beings. Marney argued that the new event of Jesus Christ was actually the old event of creation itself. However, this time around the human race stood to gain more than it had ever lost after the fall into sin. Like the apostle Paul, Marney claimed that what is to be gained in a new humanity in Christ far exceeds what had been lost in the old creation in Adam and Eve. With Jesus Christ we finally have come to accept our humanness, and we are prepared to work with all the human potential God has given us.

Creation and Christ go hand in hand to provide the essential keys for the fulfillment of our humanity. Christ remains for Marney the redemptive work of God in the life of human beings. It is through God's gracious love in Christ that we are made whole again (salvation). Being made in God's image was a great affirmation of our original creation by God, but the presence of Jesus Christ in human history is even a further climactic step toward our humanization. Marney summarized his views on creation and Christ by quoting one of his favorite theologians, Sören Kierkegaard: "Why are all of you content to live in the cellar when there are rooms upstairs?"[17] Creation in God's image was a profound challenge for human beings to live upstairs with dignity and with a strong sense of personal worth. Jesus Christ was indeed the human race's "unexploited advantage" which confirmed this ultimate possibility.

The Value of the Church

The church of Jesus Christ is a fellowship of people who seek to realize their full humanity in the name of their Lord and Savior. It was within the context of the church that Marney discovered his living laboratory. Here he could challenge people to growth and maturity as they sought to fulfill their calling as sons and daughters of a living God. The church was to be a place for people, people struggling with difficult questions— what does it mean to be truly human in God's eyes? and how can Christian discipleship be lived out in relation to others?

Marney was not interested in church structure or organization. He did not like ecclesiastical games, and he had no taste for denominational politics. In fact, he had some grave misgivings about the organized church in America. He wrote: "As for myself, I have less and less hope that denominational houses can offer any redemption for us. Indeed, most times, as formerly, the institutional church seems somehow in the way."[18] Marney believed the church's future was to be found among informal groups within the church who were willing to live in a "community of relation" as the church, but without all the trappings of denominationalism. He envisioned the future church as a gathering of people willing to risk themselves by becoming vulnerable to one another through the asking of tough questions— questions which would challenge and stretch their faith.[19]

Marney's vision of the church as a "community of relation" was stimulated by the lessons he learned from the people he served in three different congregations. The first church Marney pastored after the completion of his education was a Baptist congregation in Paducah, Kentucky. This church was located in a rural pocket of poverty and many of the members of the town's Baptist church were quite poor. Here Marney said it was his privilege to meet many good, common folks. Later he wrote, "I learned all I know about poverty, hope, and native dignity in a huge old church in Paducah."[20]

The First Baptist Church of Austin, Texas, taught Marney another lesson about the human spirit. This second church served by Marney was very different from the first. In Austin he was confronted by powerful politicians and strong-willed civic leaders; the governor and several legislators sat regularly in the congregation of First Baptist, Austin. It was an exciting and invigorating place to be, but Marney soon discovered the ugly specter of racism in the Austin community and within his church. As much as he, his wife, and two daughters loved Texas, he knew he could not overlook these racial problems. Marney went to work. He gathered with congregational leaders and with civic leaders from outside the church. Together they met the challenge of racism and headed off thirteen new pieces of racist legislation at the state capital.[21] Marney had discovered that people can change and prejudices can be addressed.

Marney's greatest challenge in the establishment of a "community of relation" came in his third and final church in Charlotte, North Carolina. When he accepted the call to the Myers Park Baptist Church, he knew he was taking on a comfortable, upper-middle-class, "country club" church. While at Myers Park, Marney stirred the conscience of his congregation and moved his people to a position of social responsibility. Members of Myers Park became more intentional about their involvement in issues which affected poor people and blacks within the greater Charlotte area. In addition, Marney challenged his congregants to personal growth; he refused to accept the complacency and apathy which often attends the lives of the wealthy and well educated.

It was at Myers Park that Marney gained a national reputation as a preacher. Guests from around the country would visit on Sunday mornings just to hear him preach. He became a speaker on the seminary and university circuit. These were indeed Marney's peak years. At Myers Park, he worked incredibly hard to gain the confidence of his congregation. Gene Owens, Marney's successor in the Myers Park pulpit, has written about Marney's relationship with the people of Myers Park.

For ten years he [Marney] fermented in Texas before coming to the Park. He swaggered in . . . trailing mud and horse manure, speaking a language few understood, swapping yarns around sophisticated camp fires, living and preaching a Gospel of tough freedom.[22]

This "Gospel of tough freedom" was an unsettling thing. Marney did not pamper his congregation; he called them to maturity in faith; he asked them to accept Jesus' lead and become free persons committed to God and one another.

Marney's challenge worked. Myers Park became a church that was happening. Unfortunately, the pastor could not keep pace. Slowed by serious illness, including a heart attack, Marney resigned from the Myers Park pulpit in 1968. He said about his departure: "I'm not a refugee from a church that wasn't happening, I'm a burnt-out hulk from a church that was happening faster than I could keep up with it."[23]

Marney, however, did not give up on his search for a "community of relation." In his last years he attempted to create a place where people could come together and teach one another about being fully human. He called his dream Interpreter's House. Located at Lake Junaluska, North Carolina, Interpreter's House served as an ecumenical way station for ministers and laity who wanted to recapture their humanity. This retreat center was another of Marney's sophisticated camp fires. Here he continued to counsel and write in what he called his self-imposed exile. Marney persisted in his pilgrimage at Interpreter's House until his death at his desk on July 5, 1978.

What Does It Mean to Be Fully Human?

By the close of Marney's life it was evident that his deepest convictions rested upon a belief in the interrelatedness of all creation. The way to the completion of our humanity was through the establishment of meaningful relations with the Creator and other human beings, as well as with other aspects of the created world. Quoting from the Jewish philosopher Martin Buber, Marney liked to say: "In the beginning is relation."[24] Drawing from biblical tradition, Marney argued that we cannot really know God apart from our relationship to God's world. The biblical

God does not stand apart; God is experienced only in relation to human history and the natural order.

This relational theology shaped and directed all of Marney's thinking about human-divine relationships. Philosophers could describe the attributes of God, as if God were a pure idea, but the God of the Bible could not be described in that fashion. Marney asserted that God was so thoroughly involved in the life of the world that it led all the way to the cross. Our model for human relations needed to follow the Creator's lead. In the final analysis we cannot become fully human until we have wrestled with the divine encounter. Or as Marney expressed it: "It is out of the experience of encounter with this Other, this Thou, that personality finds its . . . major bases. . . ."[25] In this assertion Marney reached far beyond the humanistic perspective with which he flirted. In the end he was convinced that our full humanity only can be expressed theologically. The key to Marney's entire quest for humanness was to be found in his most elemental conviction: we are indeed made in God's image, and we are indeed completed in the new creation of Jesus Christ.

Should we desire to be fully human, then we must be released from our own self-imposed prisons. We should not be afraid to reach out to others. We should expect to encounter God in our midst. In short, we need to be willing to take risks. People might even think us odd. As with Marney, our views and actions might make us "characters" in some people's eyes, but we must persist. Our meaning as human beings is incomplete without significant contact with others and with God. Above all else, Carlyle Marney has demonstrated to us that we need each other for the completion of our own humanity. In the language of the Christian faith we are called to be "Christ" to one another. In this way a new and wonderful world of relationships between humanity and humanity's Creator can once again be opened.

Recommended Readings

Carlyle Marney
The Coming Faith. Nashville: Abingdon Press, 1970.
The Recovery of the Person. Nashville: Abingdon Press, 1979.
Structures of Prejudice. Nashville: Abingdon Press, 1961.

Books about Carlyle Marney

Carey, John J., *Carlyle Marney: A Pilgrim's Progress*. Macon, Georgia: Mercer University Press, 1980.

NOTES

[1] This thought was shared by Marney with many people, especially in the context of his counseling with clergy groups.

[2] Carlyle Marney, *The Recovery of the Person* (Nashville: Abingdon Press, 1979), pp. 25-26.

[3] *Ibid.*, p. 32.

[4] Mary Kratt, ed., *Marney* (Charlotte, N.C.: Myers Park Baptist Church, 1979), p. 60.

[5] This comment about Marney's powerful voice was made to me by the Reverend Jack Hodges of McMinnville, Oregon, and I'm sure it was the opinion of many others as well.

[6] Mary Kratt, ed., *Marney*, p. 13.

[7] Carlyle Marney, *Structures of Prejudice* (Nashville: Abingdon Press, 1961), p. 244.

[8] Mary Kratt, ed., *Marney*, p. 16.

[9] This story was told to me by the Reverend Bernard Turner of McMinnville, Oregon. The pastor in the story is not Mr. Turner.

[10] Mary Kratt, ed., *Marney*, p. 43.

[11] *Ibid.*, p. 78.

[12] This dialogue transpired during a visit by Carlyle Marney to the Linfield College campus in McMinnville, Oregon, in the spring of 1978.

[13] Carlyle Marney, *The Recovery of the Person*, p. 130.

[14] *Ibid.*, p. 102.

[15] Carlyle Marney, *Faith in Conflict* (Nashville: Abingdon Press, 1957), pp. 36-39.

[16] Carlyle Marney, *The Coming Faith* (Nashville: Abingdon Press, 1970), p. 33.

[17] Marney, *Faith in Conflict*, p. 116.

[18] Marney, *The Recovery of the Person*, p. 100.

[19] Marney's discussion of a "community of relation" can be found in *The Recovery of the Person*, Part Three, Chapter 2, "The Crucible of Identification."

[20] Carlyle Marney, "Dayton's Long Hot Summer: A Memoir," in *The Scopes Trial: Forty Years After*, ed. Gerry Thompkins (New York: Charles Scribner's Sons, 1965), quoted in John J. Carey, *Carlyle Marney: A Pilgrim's Progress* (Macon, Ga.: Mercer University Press, 1980), p. 30.

[21] *Ibid.*, p. 34.

[22] Mary Kratt, ed., *Marney*, p. 7.

[23] *Ibid.*, p. 89.

[24] Martin Buber, *I and Thou*, trans. Ronald G. Smith (New York: Charles Scribner's Sons; London: T. and T. Clark, n.d.), p. 18, quoted in Marney, *Structures of Prejudice*, p. 219.

[25] *Ibid.*

3

HOWARD THURMAN:
How Do We Experience
the Presence of God?

Whither shall I go from thy Spirit?
Or whither shall I flee from thy
  presence?
If I ascend to heaven, thou art there!
If I make my bed in Sheol, thou
  art there!
If I take the wings of the morning
  and dwell in the uttermost parts
  of the sea,
even there thy hand shall lead me,
  and thy right hand shall hold me.
If I say, "Let only darkness cover me,
  and the light about me be night,"
even the darkness is not dark to thee,
  the night is bright as the day;
  for darkness is as light with thee.
  —Psalm 139:7-12

How do we experience the presence of God? The psalmist's answer was clear and certain. We experience God's Spirit wherever we are; there is literally no place where we can flee from the hand of God. Why, then, do we often feel abandoned by the Divine? Perhaps abandoned is too strong a term for some of us. We may simply experience the absence of God. Our attitude might be: God may very well be present, but God is not present *for me.* Many of us can say, "I know that the Bible speaks of the presence of God, but I have not experienced this encounter for myself."

49

There is in our world today a widespread spiritual vacuum. Many of us know of an emptiness that reaches to the very depths of our being. We want to believe, but even more importantly we want to experience something. We want this "something" to touch the numbness of our hearts and the weariness of our minds. We would like more than anything else to rediscover the spiritual dimension within our lives. The problem, in fact, may be with us rather than with God. If the psalmist is right in his assertion that the Divine is always present, then perhaps we have lost our ability to recognize that presence. The real problem may not be the absence of God; it may be the loss of consciousness on our part of the Divine Presence. God is present; the problem is that we are not present to God!

We have lost our awareness of the presence of God. Things may have become too mechanized, or perhaps we have been distracted by the management of our material possessions. We may also have acquiesced to an excessive rationalism which discredits anything that cannot be weighed or measured. For whatever the reasons, our ability to sense God's presence has been dulled if not extinguished. We now have to work consciously to recover our spiritual sensibilities. In an earlier age we might have had fewer distractions, but today everything and everybody competes for our attention.

What is the way out of our spiritual malaise? One answer is to find a spiritual guide—someone who has maintained a living awareness of the Divine Presence, someone who can point the way for us in our own struggles to recapture a personal relationship with God. Howard Thurman was this kind of individual. No religious thinker in our century has been more attuned to the quest for God than this genuinely humble man. By examining the life and thoughts of Howard Thurman, we may very well discover new ways to experience an old truth—the living presence of God.

"Twentieth-Century Holy Man"

In the year 1910 Halley's comet streaked through the skies of Daytona Beach, Florida. Everyone worried about what might happen if this giant specter should collide with the earth. Howard Thurman, then a young boy, can remember asking his mother what would become of them if this disaster occurred. His mother, equally frightened, nevertheless managed a steady and confident response, "Nothing will happen to us Howard, God will take care of us."[1] This story, recorded in Thurman's autobiography *With Head and Heart*, is illustrative of a basic, almost primordial trust Thurman's mother placed in God. It was this kind of elemental affirmation of faith that Thurman himself would seek throughout his life. In his mind and in his heart he searched for a God whose presence could reveal the joy and mystery of divine encounter.

There are some basic facts we should know as we begin to map the spiritual journey of Howard Thurman. He was born in 1900 and he died in 1981. He is best known for his accomplishments as the co-founding pastor of the first truly integrated church in the United States, the Church of the Fellowship of All Peoples, established in San Francisco in 1944. Thurman also made his reputation as the dean of the chapel at Howard University and Boston University. While at Boston he became the first black to hold a full-time faculty appointment at that university.

Thurman is remembered by many as a great preacher. At midcentury *Life* magazine recognized Dr. Thurman as one of the twelve greatest preachers in modern American life. His friendship with Martin Luther King, Jr., and Mahatma Gandhi placed him among historic company. Writing in *Ebony* magazine in 1978, Lerone Bennett spoke for thousands of admirers when he referred to Howard Thurman as a "Twentieth Century Holy Man." Many people sensed a special spiritual quality in this quiet, gifted man. He appeared to be a man in touch with both himself and God. He was serene, but not in a passive way. There was a contagious vitality about the man; the fluid gestures of his hands and dancing penetration of his eyes were extremely engaging.

It was my privilege to meet Howard Thurman in 1978. Dr. Thurman had come to our college campus as a speaker and it was my responsibility to host this gracious individual. We spent a special moment together one evening as we walked across the

campus grounds. As we strolled, I noticed that neither of us
had spoken for some time. Thurman, I'm sure, was much more
comfortable with the silence than I was. His gaze was fixed upon
the evening stars. I waited in silence for my guest to speak;
somehow it seemed inappropriate to interrupt this purposeful
silence. Then, with his gentle voice, he ended the quiet time.
Gesturing with his hands, he professed, "There is something
about the night; it is a very special time, it is my favorite time."
After a lengthy pause, he continued, "I feel closer to things at
night—you can sense a Presence all about you."[2]

One year later it suddenly dawned on me what Howard Thurman had revealed to me that magic evening together on our
campus. I confess that I had initially taken his comments to be
of no consequence. Now I realized that Dr. Thurman had shared
a significant piece of his own spiritual experience with me. We
had shared together in an intimate moment of divine encounter.

Howard Thurman had that kind of effect upon people. He
helped others find their own spiritual bearings. He was able to
introduce hundreds, if not thousands, to their own personal
sense of God's presence. Sue Bailey Thurman has said of her
husband that he was a man who knew how to call other people
home. He had an innate sense that all of life shared a common
spiritual ground. He believed that outside our rigid adherence
to religious doctrines and beyond our defense of a particular
religion or philosophy, we can find a universal mutuality. But
as we shall see, the road to this common ground was a difficult
and dangerous venture for Thurman.

The Search for Common Ground

Howard Thurman's search for common ground began early
in his childhood. As a black raised in Daytona Beach, Florida,
at the beginning of this century, he learned quickly that there
was literally no common ground between blacks and whites in
his hometown. The tentacles of racism reached into every area
of the community's activities. Racist policies in the Daytona
schools prevented blacks from receiving a high school education.
Blacks were graduated from the seventh grade and denied access
to the eighth grade. This kept them from acquiring the eighth

grade diploma which was necessary for entrance into high school.

Fortunately, Thurman was able to circumvent this racist obstacle with the help of his grade school principal. His principal privately tutored him until he was prepared to challenge the eighth grade examination and thereby receive an eighth grade diploma. However, once he had the diploma in hand, the possibility of a high school education was still remote. There were only three public high schools for blacks in the entire state of Florida.[3] Since none of these schools was near Daytona Beach, a public high school education was not possible. But Thurman was not to be denied his education. He enrolled in a private, church-related black high school in nearby Jacksonville. His family worked hard to pay the tuition. Thurman, in turn, studied and worked to the point of physical exhaustion, but his effort was well worth it. He graduated first in his class and received a scholarship to Morehouse College, but this was not the end of Thurman's formal education. He attended Colgate Rochester Divinity School where he again graduated number one in his class. The educational roadblocks had been overcome.

Other racist obstacles, however, were more difficult to surmount. The daily indignities which black children faced in the racist South were constant reminders to Thurman that he was a nonperson in the white world. He writes in his autobiography:

> I was a very sensitive child who suffered much from the violences of racial conflict. The climate of our town, Daytona Beach, Florida, was better than most Southern towns because of the influence of the tourists who wintered there. Nevertheless, life became more and more suffocating because of the fear of being brutalized, beaten, or otherwise outraged.[4]

Young Howard experienced frequent assaults upon his dignity as a human being. A harmless activity like raking leaves could become a racial incident. Thurman remembers that on one occasion he was attacked by a five-year-old white girl when he scolded her for scattering the pile of leaves he had just raked. In anger, the girl had drawn a straight-pin from her dress and had stabbed him in the hand. Thurman said he reeled back in pain and asked the girl why she had done such a thing. Then came the devastating reply, "Oh, Howard, that didn't hurt you! You can't feel!"[5]

The racist assumption of the white child was clear. Howard Thurman was a black "boy" and everyone knew that blacks could not feel pain like whites. Blacks cannot feel pain because blacks are not human—this was the real point! Certainly in this kind of social climate it was difficult, if not impossible, to find common ground with other human beings. This kind of racism prevented any sense of commonality within the social and cultural setting of Thurman's racially divided homeland.

Finding Companionship in the Divine

It was clear that Thurman's social world lacked common ground; so he turned to the world of nature in search of harmony. Nature became Thurman's open-air cathedral, and the wonders of the natural world seemed to carry him beyond the boundaries of racial prejudice and bigotry. He has reported that his earliest childhood memories are related to his delightful encounters with the natural world. These were pleasant memories, and they differed from the fears and apprehensions which attended the social world of Daytona Beach. He discovered nature to be his friend.

Thurman tells us that he was befriended by the woods near his home. The ocean also became one of his joyful companions. He even had his own secret hiding place, the oak tree in his backyard. This tree became Thurman's most trusted boyhood friend. He has said of his friend, "I needed the strength of that tree, and, like it, I wanted to hold my ground. . . . I could reach down in the quiet places of my spirit, take out my bruises and my joys, unfold them and talk about them."[6] In his communion with the oak tree, Thurman knew that he was understood.

This feeling of close fellowship also extended to other aspects of the natural world. It can be said that Thurman had his first experiences of God in the natural world. He did not have words for it but he sensed a powerful connection between his spirit and something wholly other. This "other" was in nature but it was not limited to nature. He wrote, "There were times when it seemed as if the earth and the river and sky and I were one beat of the same pulse." Then, he added, "There would come a moment when beyond the single pulse beat there was a sense of Presence which seemed to speak to me."[7] In this Presence, Thurman encountered a source or a reality which he believed to be' the very center of all life; it was understood to be a kind of dynamic power in which we live, move, and have our being. He has written of these luminous events, "There was no voice. There was no image. There was no vision. There was God."[8]

As we have already noted, Thurman also had a keen sense of this Presence at nighttime. His fascination for the night seemed to extend beyond the scope of his intimate relationship with other natural phenomena. He found genuine comfort in the night. In one of Thurman's most revealing passages, he writes:

> Nightfall was meaningful to my childhood, for the night was more than a companion. It was a presence, an articulate climate. There was something about the night that seemed to cover my spirit like a gentle blanket. . . . [9]

Even in childhood, Thurman had sensed that beyond race, beyond culture, and beyond religion there was the simple and undeniable fact of the self before an intimate Presence.

Out of His Roots

This intimate Presence discovered by Thurman was also to be found in his religious experience within the black church. Here, without hesitation, the believers called that Presence "God." At the Mount Bethel Baptist Church, Thurman was told that he was a "somebody" because he was loved by the God who created us all. He learned that what he did with his life was important to the people of Mount Bethel. They cared about him as one of God's precious creations.[10] In the worship and fellowship of the congregation, Thurman sensed a personal Reality which was much akin to the Presence he knew in nature. In the church context, this Presence was worshiped as the God of Abraham and Sarah, and the God of Jesus Christ.

Yet, even in the church there was no escape from racism. Blacks in Daytona Beach were not permitted to worship in white churches. They were required to keep to their "own kind." For example, as a young boy Thurman was "allowed" to pump the church organ for the Episcopal organist during weekday practices, but on Sundays, the sacred time of the week, he was replaced at the organ pump by a white boy. The message was clear: The sacred time of white people could not be defiled by the presence of blacks. This outraged Thurman. Such affronts to his spirit were extremely difficult to endure.[11]

Thurman's grandmother, however, gave him another perspective on this kind of psychological violence. Born a slave, she had a keen sense of what really counted in life. She guarded and nurtured young Howard's sensitive spirit. According to Thurman, whenever his spirit hit rock bottom, his grandmother would buoy him up with a story from her slave days on the plantation. In her favorite story she would recount for Thurman how once a year a slave preacher was permitted to preach to the slaves. The slave preacher would deliver a powerful sermon which always ended the same way. Without flinching, the slave preacher would look his congregation square in the eye and declare with all the force he could muster, "You are not niggers! You are not slaves! You are God's children!"[12]

This was an important theological discovery for Thurman. It was a lesson that he would never forget. He was a child of God. No person, or no group of people, could take that away from him. As a child of God, he was freed of all racist definitions of his being. He was a somebody because he belonged only to God. No individual had the right to define him as a nonperson. He had been given a tremendous spiritual insight; he was a child of God.

During his high school years this particular child of God declared that he had been called by God to the ministry. In describing his calling, he said, ". . . there was the clear pull and insistence of the Spirit of God within my own heart, urging me to say Yes to the Light and to trust God with and for the results."[13] However, Thurman's yes to God was qualified by serious reservations concerning the church. Although his church experience had been positive for the most part, there was one event which nearly turned him against this institution forever. When Thurman was only seven years old, his father was stricken by a fever and died. The tragedy of this untimely death was exacerbated by the Mount Bethel Baptist Church, which refused to bury Saul Thurman because he was not a member. Thurman's grandmother was outraged, and she put pressure on the church to reverse its decision. The deacons finally agreed to permit the burial, but the Thurmans were instructed to find their own minister for the funeral rites. Unfortunately the only preacher available was a traveling evangelist by the name of Sam Cromarte.

The funeral was a disaster! Cromarte preached a "hellfire and brimstone" sermon; the object of this vitriolic sermon was Thurman's father. Howard Thurman has written of this disastrous event, "I listened with wonderment, then anger, and finally mounting rage as Sam Cromarte preached my father into hell."[14] Thurman's spirit was wrenched by the violence of this kind of preaching. His father's dignity had been violated by a man who did not even know Saul Thurman. In blind rage he vowed on the spot never to have anything to do with the church when he became an adult.

For many years, Thurman was troubled by what the church and Sam Cromarte had done to his father's memory. He was faced with a genuine conflict. How could he provide leadership for the church? It had refused to bury his father and, furthermore, it produced men like Cromarte. Thurman struggled with this issue even as he prepared for the ministry in seminary. He finally resolved the issue by committing himself to changing the church. He was determined to create the kind of fellowship which would be inclusive rather than exclusive. He would not act toward others in the way that the Mount Bethel church had acted toward his father.

In the 1940s Thurman was able to realize his dream; he helped found the Church of the Fellowship of All Peoples in San Francisco. This unique church became Thurman's living testimony to inclusive fellowship. Asians, blacks, and whites shared in the leadership of Fellowship Church, and no person was excluded because of race or creed. Thurman would not accept exclusivist or segregationist claims made in the name of religion. Exclusion in theological matters of salvation was as intolerable to him as exclusion for reasons of race. A theological doctrine which saved some and damned others was as bigoted in his estimate as the social doctrine of racism. The division of the human race into "us" and "them" was wrong in any case. Without question, Thurman's personal experience with social and religious exclusivism shaped the direction of his public ministry. In opposition to all forms of exclusivism, he chose to champion the integration of human life at all levels—the social, political, and spiritual!

The Way of the Mystic

Thurman's commitment to an inclusive way of life led him to the path of mysticism. By definition, a mystic is a person who seeks a personal and direct relationship with God through spiritual discipline. Thurman had always been a mystic by natural inclination, but he had not yet been exposed to the spiritual theology of mystics. This exposure to the academic side of mysticism came about when he met Rufus Jones, the great Quaker mystic and scholar. Thurman knew nothing about Jones until he happened to stumble upon Jones's book *Finding the Trail of Life* at a church convention. He was intrigued by the title and so he sat down on the steps of the convention's host church to read. He was captivated by Jones's insights. Thurman later recalled, "I did not move until I had read the entire book. When I finished, I knew that if this man were alive, I wanted to study with him."[15]

Rufus Jones was indeed alive; so in 1927 Thurman took leave from his church in Oberlin, Ohio, and set off for Haverford College in Pennsylvania to study with the Quaker mystic. There he spent a semester of independent study as a graduate student in Jones's seminars. He and Jones formed an immediate bond of friendship. Although Jones was much Thurman's senior, the two shared the same intense interest in the study of religious experience. Both men had a deep passion for exploring life in its interior dimensions. Thurman discovered that Jones's philosophy confirmed some of his own most basic convictions. For example, Jones taught that the personal experience of God had an unavoidable ethical consequence. The true mystic could not withdraw from life. Quite the contrary was true. The experiences of God in the inner self caused the mystic to have compassion for all of life. The mystic is challenged to love every human being. According to Thurman:

He [Jones] gave to me confidence in the insight that the religion of the inner life could deal with the empirical experience of man without retreating from the demands of such experience. To state what I mean categorically, the religion of the inner life at its best is life affirming rather than life denying. . . . [16]

Thurman learned from Jones's Quaker tradition that a sense of social responsibility is directly related to the guidance of an individual's "inner light." Thurman had found confirmation for his belief that the inner spiritual life and the outer moral life were inseparable.

Thurman's study with Jones helped bring his own life into sharper focus. He has said of this period, "I have sought a way of life that could come under the influence of, and be informed by, the fruits of the inner life."[17] Jones had given Thurman an intellectual framework for fitting the pieces of his life together. What Thurman had known with his heart, he now understood with his mind. He was confident that the way of the mystic was not a form of religious escapism. The development of the inner life led directly to responsible and creative living in the world. Thurman said that he had learned how "to live under siege, with the equilibrium and tranquility of peace . . ."[18]

He could now carry on his public ministry with courage and determination because he had found access to the inner peace essential for the survival of his own being. Thurman also transmitted this valuable lesson to his students and friends. He reminded them that the spiritual quest involved both the inner and outer dimensions of human life. Those who truly seek to know and to love God will also seek to know and to love neighbor. These two tasks are mutually dependent one upon the other. This lesson was learned well by Thurman's most famous student and friend, Martin Luther King, Jr. Thurman took great pride in the knowledge that King had carried his book *Jesus and the Disinherited* into the civil rights marches of the 1960s.[19]

Disciplines of the Spirit

Thurman believed that the inner life needed to be fed by the Spirit of God. Without this nurturing, the human spirit could not grow strong. He taught that as God's children we must keep attuned to the stirrings of God's Spirit within our own souls. If we as individuals paid closer attention to the signals within, we might discover an opening for communion with God's Spirit. Thurman proposed that spiritual disciplines could help us get in touch with this inward truth. In his book *The Creative Encounter*, he writes, ". . . there is present in religious experience an original and direct element which seems to be in, and of itself, intrinsic and supremely worthful."[20] In other words, we human beings are by nature religious. Perhaps an even better word for it is "spiritual." Being spiritual does not necessarily mean that we have special gifts, like a good ear for music or a creative, artistic hand. In Thurman's estimate, every person has an innate spiritual awareness of the Divine Presence. No special talents or gifts are necessary; we do not have to be spiritual virtuosos.

If Thurman is correct and we all have a spiritual dimension, why is it then that we all do not recognize God's Presence? The answer is that we have been distracted from our spiritual selves. Our lives have been dulled through our own lack of awareness of things internal and eternal. Therefore, argues Thurman, spiritual disciplines are necessary to help us regain our own lost consciousness of the Divine. Spiritual disciplines are not meant to manufacture religious experience; however, they are meant to uncover the religious experience which is present in our lives but buried in our own self-distractions. Disciplines of the spirit can help us recover our spirituality, and they may even enhance our spiritual sensitivities.

According to Thurman, spiritual disciplines can include many things, the use of Scripture, the examination of devotional writings, the practice of prayer and meditation, the establishment of certain physical exercises, and so forth. The major discipline which Thurman emphasized was the practice of silence. He believed that an individual must be willing to listen, really listen, before he or she speaks. A person must be willing to "wait upon the Lord." Borrowing a phrase from Quaker tradition, Thurman encouraged his students to "center down." This means to get quiet so that if God speaks, God can be heard.

Like other spiritual disciplines, "centering down" requires

that certain practical steps be taken. Thurman advised that those who practiced silence should "seek a physical place of withdrawal."[21] He himself was careful to set aside special times and special locations for quiet meditation. He knew that he needed time apart and he encouraged others to find their own quiet moments. Thurman suggested that we take a walk, or remain in bed after everyone else is up, or withdraw from active conversation for a short time. Above all, he said we should find the silent discipline which best suits our own needs and our own personalities.

From Thurman's perspective, the practice of silence leads to an even more essential discipline: the practice of prayer. He understood prayer to be more than a conversation between the self and God. Prayer is the very heartbeat of our spiritual existence. In this sense, prayer is understood to be a complete way of life; it involves our entire orientation toward the Divine. Prayer, for Thurman, was a process, and it had to be viewed as a living continuum. He wrote:

> Prayer is not only the participation in communication with God in the encounter of religious experience, but it is also the "readying" of the spirit for such communication. It is the total process of quieting down and to that extent must not be separated from meditation.[22]

Prayer, then, involves quieting down, listening, and sensing the presence of God's Spirit. When our spirit meets the Divine Spirit, prayer begins in earnest.

Our life of prayer, in Thurman's view, could be enhanced by a reliance upon our religious traditions. Christians can be helped in their prayers by beginning with phrases from the Old and New Testaments. In fact, Christians have many models for praying, including the Psalms and the simple prayer which Jesus taught his disciples. Jews, on the other hand, can begin with prayers drawn from their rabbinic tradition, and they can turn to the Torah and Talmud. Buddhists might begin their prayers with a meditation on the Buddha, and Muslims can certainly find starters for prayers in the Quran. In any case, Thurman advises that we begin to pray from our own religious "idiom."

He also invites us to discover some "spiritual clothesline" on which to hang our prayers. It is important to have our favorite starting point from which we can reach down into our deepest selves. In Thurman's case his "spiritual clothesline" was Psalm 139. The opening line of this psalm became his prayer lead. "O Lord, thou hast searched me and known me!"[23] From this starting point he was able to let his thoughts spring forth and flow wherever they might lead him.

Prayer was always an opening for Thurman, a little window to the soul and a larger window to God. He believed that prayer brought him as close as he could come to his Creator; it focused his attention on the Creator's world. Rather than asking for God's help, Thurman envisioned prayer as a way of preparing us to serve in God's world. Therefore, the discipline of prayer is viewed as an act of commitment in which we approach life from God's perspective rather than from our own. Prayer is a commitment to look for wholeness in life, to find our common life together in God's realm.

A Follower of Jesus

Thurman's model for spiritual discipline and commitment was Jesus Christ. According to Dr. Thurman, "He who seeks God with all of his heart will someday on his way meet Jesus."[24] He recognized that while all may not choose to follow Jesus, none could ignore the power of his spiritual presence and his closeness to God. In line with these thoughts, Thurman decided to approach the life of Jesus from the standpoint of Jesus' spirituality, that is, from the perspective of Jesus' relation to God. In Jesus, Thurman discovered a spiritual vitality that he considered to be highly contagious. He observed: "Jesus approached all of life from within the tremendous vitality of his religious experience."[25]

Childhood experiences in the black church had taught Thurman about the reality of a living Christ. He spoke often of his early encounter with Jesus under the old oak tree and elsewhere. He was absolutely serious about the presence of Jesus' Spirit in his life, and he wrote about it without pious pretense.[26] It was simply a fact of life for him. Long before he learned about doctrines of Christology, he had experienced for himself the personal meaning of God's love in the Spirit of Jesus.

In his teaching about Jesus Christ, Thurman wanted to push back behind ecclesiastical doctrines of Christ to the historical Jesus of first-century Palestine. According to Thurman, the historic dogmas of Christianity had substituted a religion *about* Jesus for the religion *of* Jesus.[27] It is the religion *of* Jesus which ought to be the focus of Jesus' followers; it is Jesus' relationship with God which presents the ultimate challenge to us. Within the Great Commandment of Jesus to love God and to love neighbor, we find the true genius of Jesus' life. Here is our call to discipleship; we are to emulate that kind of love and total dedication.

However, the church has by and large missed the point. We worship Jesus, but we do not follow the way of Jesus' life. Thurman notes that Christianity has often robbed Jesus of his religious vitality by failing to recall the historical facts of his life. First, Jesus was a Jew. Second, Jesus was a poor Jew. Third, Jesus was a poor Jew who was a member of a minority group within the ancient Greco-Roman world.[28] All these historical factors affected Jesus' religious experience, just as they influenced the entirety of his life. By forgetting that Jesus was a poor Jew in a world controlled by the powerful Romans, we lose sight of the significance of the incarnation (the in-fleshment of God in this particular human being).

In his book *Jesus and the Disinherited*, Thurman argues that Jesus' entire view of God and humanity was shaped by his experience as a poor, oppressed Jew. If we are to find God in Jesus, then we must be open to viewing life from the perspective of Jesus' lowly position. In Thurman's opinion, Jesus has demonstrated God's special concern for those who have no voice in society. Jesus championed the cause of the disinherited. It was in the midst of his people's own oppression that Jesus dared to offer a startling solution for their problems. Thurman called it a "creative solution." Rather than the use of war and more repression, Jesus pointed to the way of love and reconciliation.

This sort of approach to life would require a tremendous moral and spiritual commitment. It meant the exercising of a love which would be grounded in suffering as well as joy. Jesus was willing to suffer and to die so that the fruits of love, an abundant life, might be realized in others. Love's ultimate requirement dictated the abandonment of violence. Jesus was to practice nonviolence in relation to all of life. Nonviolent love was the only true weapon that the disinherited had. This was the only creative and redemptive way to meet the brutalities of the oppressors. Thurman was absolutely certain that Jesus held to this philosophy. He wrote:

> From my investigation and study, the religion of Jesus projected a creative solution to the pressing problem of survival for the minority of which He was a part in the Greco-Roman world. . . . Jesus Christ is on the side of freedom, liberty, and justice for all people, black, white, red, yellow, saint, sinner, rich, or poor.[29]

The creative solution was indeed love, and Thurman would not retreat from Jesus' high calling to nonviolence. Even during the times of our recent history when some have found violence to be a justified reaction to oppression, Thurman refused to give up his personal commitment to the loving, nonviolent approach of Jesus. Much like the Christ he followed, Thurman remained an individual of compassionate long-suffering throughout his life. He was determined to operate out of his own creative center of loving nonviolence, regardless of what others might choose to do.

How Do We Experience the Presence of God?

As we have seen Howard Thurman committed his total life's energy to the pursuit of a kind of religious experience that would place all humanity on common ground—a common ground of love and mutual respect. He has taught us much about what this experience contains. In the first place, we have learned that no individual or group can possess the total truth about God. Thurman's own experience of God's Presence is so rich and varied that we can only conclude there are many ways to encounter the living God. Whether we speak of Thurman's experience of the Divine in nature; or his encounter with God in the Christian faith of his grandmother; or the personal Jesus he met in his black religion; or the Presence he discovered in mysticism; we are constantly referring to the same Reality. The fabric of Thurman's life is tightly woven by a fine common thread, and that thread is the conviction that we are all children of the same benevolent Creator. This is the nonnegotiable "fact" of our creation. It permeates every corner of our existence, and it is the pervasive theme of Thurman's life.

In the second place, Thurman has taught us that all of life is related to its ultimate source, God. Brooding over the vastness of creation is a Presence which Thurman knew instinctively and clearly to be the Lord of the universe. Since childhood he sensed that there was a Reality which neither time nor circumstance could alter. This Reality was always present, always involved, and involving! All we need is the consciousness to recognize it. The truth of God, said Thurman, ". . . is not peculiar to any one religion but is shared by many; and it is through religion that this universal insight may be made available to the believer."[30] Accordingly, Thurman's vision is broad and inclusive, but it also has spiritual depth. He has avoided the temptation to combine all religions into a meaningless mishmash, and he cautions that we must not mistake religion for the religious experience itself. He wrote: "This is not to say that all religions are one and the same, but it is to say that the essence of the religious experience is unique, comprehensible and not dilimiting."[31] In other words, the truth which we experience at the heart of our own religion has a universal connection with all of life.

This leads to a third lesson. With Thurman's guidance, we have come to the humble recognition that our understanding of God is always constrained by our limited ability to comprehend ultimate reality. When we ask the question of how we experience God, it is important to respond—only in part. Spiritual disciplines may make us more aware of God's Presence, but even they have their limitations. Not long before his death, Thurman reiterated a truth which was the touchstone of his life. He told his friend Lerone Bennett:

. . . I think that the important thing that makes my life in some ways highly difficult to understand is that my first religious experiences always transcended the context in which they took place. And the best categorical statement on that—and I don't know when I discovered this, but I don't remember when I didn't know it—is that the things that are true in religion, in my religion, are to be found in my religion because they are true—they are not true because they are in my religion.[32]

For Howard Thurman, the living God known to Christians in Jesus Christ was also to be discovered in the collective spiritual experience of the human race. The challenge to experience and to know God knew no ultimate boundaries for Thurman. It was in this common experience of the Divine that Thurman found his spiritual home. This fact, and this fact alone, explains the boundless energy and joyful spirit of this remarkable man. Should we dare to live with a similar kind of openness and fascination for life, we too might grow to know God's Presence in an unending variety of experiences.

Recommended Readings

Howard Thurman

Creative Encounter. New York: Harper & Row, Publishers, Inc., 1954.

Disciplines of the Spirit. New York: Harper & Row, Publishers, Inc., 1963.

With Head and Heart. New York: Harcourt, Brace, Jovanovich, 1979.

NOTES

[1] Howard Thurman, *With Head and Heart* (New York: Harcourt, Brace, Jovanovich, 1979), p. 16.
[2] This event took place on the occasion of my meeting with Dr. Thurman at Linfield College in Oregon during the spring semester of 1978.
[3] Thurman, *With Head and Heart*, p. 24.
[4] Howard Thurman, *Footprints of a Dream* (New York: Harper & Row, Publishers, Inc., 1959), p. 16.
[5] Thurman, *With Head and Heart*, p. 12.
[6] *Ibid.*, pp. 8–9.
[7] Howard Thurman, *Disciplines of the Spirit* (New York: Harper & Row, Publishers, Inc. 1963), p. 96.
[8] *Ibid.*
[9] Thurman, *With Head and Heart*, p. 7.
[10] *Ibid.*, p. 20.
[11] Howard Thurman, *The Luminous Darkness* (New York: Harper & Row, Publishers, Inc., 1965), p. 11.
[12] Thurman, *With Head and Heart*, p. 21.
[13] Thurman, *Footprints of a Dream*, p. 18.
[14] Thurman, *With Head and Heart*, p. 6.

[15] *Ibid.*, p. 74.

[16] Howard Thurman, *Mysticism and the Experience of Love*, Pendle Hill Pamphlet 115 (Wallingford, Pa.: Pendle Hill, 1961), p. 3.

[17] *Ibid.*, p. 5.

[18] *Ibid.*

[19] Thurman, *With Head and Heart*, p. 255.

[20] Howard Thurman, *The Creative Encounter* (New York: Harper & Row, Publishers, Inc., 1954), p. 23.

[21] Thurman, *Disciplines of the Spirit*, p. 98.

[22] Thurman, *Creative Encounter*, p. 34.

[23] *Ibid.*, p. 36.

[24] Howard Thurman, *Deep Is the Hunger* (New York: Harper & Row, Publishers, Inc., 1951), p. 176.

[25] Howard Thurman, *The Growing Edge* (New York: Harper & Row, Publishers, Inc., 1956), p. 104.

[26] Elizabeth Yates, *Portrait of a Practical Dreamer* (New York: The John Day Company, 1964), p. 37–38.

[27] Howard Thurman, *Jesus and the Disinherited* (Nashville: Abingdon Press, 1949) includes a more detailed discussion of Thurman's distinction between the religion about Jesus and the religion of Jesus.

[28] Thurman, *Jesus and the Disinherited*, pp. 15–18.

[29] Thurman, *With Head and Heart*, p. 114.

[30] Thurman, *The Growing Edge*, p. 176.

[31] Thurman, *With Head and Heart*, p. 121.

[32] Lerone Bennett, "Howard Thurman: Twentieth Century Holy Man," *Ebony*, February, 1978. p. 76.

4

VIRGINIA MOLLENKOTT:
Is God Male or Female?

> For my thoughts are not your thoughts,
>   neither are your ways my ways, says the LORD.
> For as the heavens are higher than the earth,
>   so are my ways higher than your ways
>   and my thoughts than your thoughts.
>   —Isaiah 55:8–9

Is God male or female? Many of us would protest that this is an inappropriate question, and in one sense we would be right. As the book of Isaiah reminds us, God cannot adequately be described in human terms—and this would include references to gender. God's ways are not our ways; the thoughts of the Almighty are not our thoughts. From this theological perspective, we recognize that to speak of God as masculine or feminine is to speak of the Divine in a metaphorical sense.

God is not literally a male or a female, so why all the fuss? The problem is this: Although we may pay lip service to the idea that God is beyond gender consideration, we nevertheless continue to speak and act is if the Almighty is masculine. We constantly use the masculine pronoun "he" in our references to the Deity. Seldom do we hear God referred to as "she." The Bible itself, growing out of a patriarchal society, presents us with a preponderance of images for God which are male-oriented. Our worship on Sunday mornings would also suggest that God is male. Our prayers and liturgies and hymns are all filled with references to God as "he" and "him." The Creator is pictured as a king, a lord, a mighty warrior, and Father of us all.

If we look at our church leadership, we also get the strong impression that God is a male deity. Men dominate the pulpits, and men sit in the seats of ecclesiastical power. Seldom is a top executive or a bishop or an archbishop a woman. Given all of this, we must ask the very painful question: What does a male-dominated church and religion have to say to women? The blunt answer is that Christianity has often functioned as a men's club which is run by men for men in a setting in which God is viewed as "one of the boys."

Fortunately, many within the church today, women and men alike, find the use of exclusive male language in reference to God to be offensive. Many Christians also refuse to perpetuate the church's image as a men's club by insisting upon equal representation between the sexes in church leadership. There is, in fact, a revolution occurring within the contemporary church. Many women are beginning to speak out in order to claim their birthright as daughters of God. Some of these voices are angry, some are measured, some are quiet, but all are filled with resolve that Christ's body, the church, should respect the role and the status of women as equal partners with men in the service of God's kingdom.

One of the most effective and instructive of these voices belongs to Virginia Ramey Mollenkott. As a contemporary evangelical Christian, she has done much to witness for the cause of women within the church and within society. Her witness is biblically based, and it drives to the theological center of the issues of sexism and exclusiveness. She is first and foremost a theologian. Her questions for the church cut through the usual political rhetoric to the theological core. Are we, for example, willing to continue to speak and act as if God is a male entity? Have we turned the Almighty God into a cultic god for men only? Will the church be able to broaden its scope to include feminine as well as masculine references to the Divine? Can the church share its leadership responsibilities equally between men and women?

These are hard questions, but they must soon be faced if the church of Jesus Christ is to maintain credibility with the female half of the world's population. With the help of Virginia Mollenkott, we can gain some helpful, and even redeeming, insights into the critical issues involved in our own struggles to understand God in a more inclusive way.

Out of Bondage

Some stories are stories of personal liberation. Such is the case with Virginia Mollenkott. Her early childhood was filled with obstacles to her social and spiritual development. To begin with, she was overweight as a child. Thirteen and a half pounds at birth, Mollenkott gained steadily through to her adult years. It was only after she had had her own child that she learned her "weight problem" had to do with a medial problem; she turned out to be hypoglycemic with a hyperinsulin reaction.[1] Under a doctor's care, she was able to lose eighty-five pounds from her all-time high.

However, in childhood the unspoken assumption was that she was fat because she lacked the willpower to push herself away from the table. She can still remember with great pain the teasing of her friends and even her family. She has written of these experiences, "I remember especially one very painful time when Dad teased me about being his little tub, and I burst into tears at this betrayal from my adored tower of strength."[2] Perhaps this incident would have been just another of the constant indignities which an overweight child must endure, but Mollenkott's father persisted in his "good-natured" kidding. According to Mollenkott:

> Not realizing how wounded I was, he teased me some more about crying, then got irritated because I didn't stop and ordered me to be a good sport and wipe my eyes. When I couldn't comply, he told me to sit in the corner for an hour—and my mother did nothing to interfere. I sat there raging with the injustice of it all.[3]

It was indeed a liberating experience for Mollenkott to discover that her fatness was not the result of her own sloth, as everyone had assumed. As a result of this experience she resolved not to stereotype people on the basis of their appearances. Reflecting on our society's prejudice against overweight people, Mollenkott

has written: "In our society, obese people are not taken
seriously."[4] She had come to realize that fat people like other
minorities, are not listened to in our culture because they are
assumed to be morally deficient. Their plight is ignored and,
even worse, it is sometimes trivialized. They simply are not
given a serious hearing.

Another obstacle to Mollenkott's early growth and development was her fundamentalist upbringing. Not that it was all
bad. She has credited the fundamentalist Plymouth Brethren
Assembly with teaching her the "surface facts" about the Bible.
As a child, she came to know the Bible frontwards and back-
wards! However, the theology which accompanied the Bible
teaching proved to be devastating for Mollenkott's young psyche.
The older she became, the greater and greater difficulty she had
reconciling her fundamentalist faith with her academic learning.
As an intelligent, sensitive young woman, she was faced with
a spiritual crisis of major proportions. She has noted:

> It is difficult for people who have not known a fundamentalist
> background to believe the basic, almost primitive struggles such a
> background can generate in fundamentalist persons as they become
> educated. What I deeply appreciate from my own background is
> that I was thoroughly grounded in the surface facts (the words
> themselves) of the Bible. For that I feel grateful to my mother and
> to various brothers at the Plymouth Brethren Assemblies. I specify
> the *brothers*, of course, because if any of the sisters knew anything
> much about the Bible, I had no way of being aware of their knowl-
> edge. Women were not permitted to preach, or pray aloud, or even
> ask questions at the Bible "readings" (interpretative sessions).[5]

This religious world held no future for Mollenkott. Her intellectual curiosity was stifled, and her spiritual life was surpressed.
The Plymouth Brethren read only the King James Version of the
Bible, and the *Scofield Reference Bible* was the only Bible com-
mentary sanctioned for use among Plymouth Brethren. It was
assumed by the Brethren that only they would reach heaven,
with the possible exception of a few fundamentalists from other
denominations who might also be admitted. In this regard,
Mollenkott has recalled, "I distinctly remember eyeing the United
Methodist Church with disdain because people sometimes
smoked on the front steps." She also remembered "the slight

jolt I felt when first I realized that Catholics considered themselves Christians."[6]

The most repressive aspect of Mollenkott's fundamentalist
background, however, was its low estimate of the worth and
value of humanity—especially women. She had been taught
that she was totally evil. And being a spiritual descendent from
Eve made her twice as evil as men. She was the same sex as the
primeval Eve who had seduced man (Adam) into disobeying
God. The Plymouth Brethren were determined to keep women
"in their place" in order to prevent such rebellious activity in
the future.

So that God might be rightly praised, Mollenkott was taught
to diminish herself. The Almighty was viewed as being so great
that all human beings, especially women, paled in comparison.
She was taught to hate her own nature; she was instructed to
understand herself as the lowliest of sinners. The concept of
God's grace and love was almost totally absent from the theological picture which she had been given. It is little wonder that
Mollenkott has confessed: '. . . I have spent tremendous energy
just trying to understand whether my deepest being is wholly
evil or whether I might dare to believe that God is truly present
in my deepest being."[7]

Virginia Mollenkott continued to wrestle with this fundamentalist theology as she prepared for a vocation as a professor of
English literature. She asked herself whether, for God to be
lifted up, human beings had to be brought low. She wondered
if the elevation of human life necessarily meant the degradation
of God. Is our relationship with the Divine based upon this type
of "seesaw" relationship? Mollenkott thought not, especially as
she examined her Bible and also began to explore the writings
of Christian humanists. She gradually became aware of another
theological perspective, one which was quite different from her
earlier fundamentalism. In this view of God and humanity, there
could be a high estimate of both God and human life; humanity
did not have to be lowered for the sake of God's elevation.[8]

Mollenkott's struggle out of her fundamentalism and its an-
tihuman theology was not easy. Her education at Bob Jones
University and her first nine years of teaching at Shelton College

were not liberating experiences. In these settings a conservative
like Billy Graham was attacked as being too liberal theologically.
On the political side of things, these campuses were strongly
anti-Communist and Carl McIntire's theories of Communist conspiracy ruled the day.[9] In fact, these schools were against more
than they were for.

Mollenkott, on the other hand, was looking for a much more
positive approach to life. It was during her preparation for her
Ph.D. in English literature at New York University that she found
a more positive world. By the time she had completed her degree
in 1965, a new direction had been charted for her life. Without
abandoning her Christian faith, she had decided to give up a
fundamentalism which she had never fully accepted. She dedicated herself to teaching in the liberal arts tradition as a Christian
whose task it was to help students to learn to "think clearly"
and "feel humanly."[10]

One final obstacle which Mollenkott had to overcome on her
way out of spiritual bondage was her marriage. While working
on her Ph.D., it had become increasingly clear to Mollenkott
that her marriage was in trouble. In her 1980 autobiography,
Speech, Silence, Action, she has recounted for us this difficult and
exhausting time in her life.

> I remember the health-wrecking tension of those Ph.D. years:
> teaching full time and chairing the English Department at Shelton
> College, taking care of a small son and being responsible for the
> washing, the ironing, bed-making, cleaning, shopping, cooking—
> the works. I remember feeling it was unfair that my husband could
> get up from dinner and watch TV all evening while I washed the
> dishes, put the baby to bed, and then cleared a place for myself
> on the kitchen table to study for my graduate courses and prepare
> for my next day's classes. I frequently worked until the wee hours,
> always struggling to shut out the sound of the incessant television.[11]

When Mollenkott tried to discuss her concerns about the ine-
quities in her marriage, her husband responded by declaring
that the problem with the marriage was *her* childishness. Her
husband's reasoning followed the line of thought prevalent in
many fundamentalist homes. He reasoned that: "Mature women,
particularly if they believed in God's Word, had no difficulty
with their subordinate role in church and home."[12] However,

this sort of repressive logic was no longer acceptable to Mollen-kott. She knew that this kind of subordination was ruining her health, and it was a rationalization for her mistreatment as a human being.

Mollenkott realized that her husband was threatened by the questions she was raising about the marriage relationship. On top of this he was uncomfortable with his wife's growth out of fundamentalism. She has written: "My gradually opening vision seemed to Fred very threatening, very wrong, very heretical."[13] She knew that her opinion in the relationship counted for very little, and as the years passed she grew further apart from her husband. In 1967 Mollenkott accepted a teaching position with William Paterson College in New Jersey, where she continues to teach today. Not long after this, the marriage ended. Mollen-kott's husband's reaction to the Kent State shootings in 1970 illustrates the marriage's impasse. Mollenkott has written of these student deaths:

> Having spent so much of my life with college-aged young people, I felt as if some of my own children had been assassinated, and I wept. Fred regarded my tears with disgust. "Crying shows that you don't believe the Bible," he said. "Why so?" I sniffled. "Be-cause the Bible says the magistrate bears no sword in vain. Those guards were only doing what God expects magistrates to do, pre-serve law and order!" I made no reply because experience had taught me replies were useless.[14]

The marriage could not be saved; there simply was no future in something which had become a nonrelationship.

With the divorce came a new sense of freedom for Virginia Mollenkott. She was no longer bound to the many things which had enslaved her. The sad experiences of her "fat" childhood years were now history. She had freed herself from the intel-lectual and spiritual restraints of fundamentalism. And the un-healthy marriage had ended. It was indeed a new day! In a renewed burst of energy, Mollenkott devoted herself to her teaching and writing. At the college where she served as pro-fessor of English Literature, she was able to settle down to academic work and a family life with her son, Paul.

The new day, however, was not complete. Mollenkott had another important theological issue with which to come to terms.

Like thousands of other women, she desired to understand what
God was saying to her about her journey out of bondage—a
bondage which had had a great deal to do with her society's
and her religion's suppression of women. What did God have
to say to women who were attempting to find their *own* way in
a world which is so male-oriented? Did God simply sanction the
world's patriarchy, or did God have a word for women as they
sought to stand on equal footing with men? Was God the kind
of God who affirmed the worth and value of each human being—
male and female alike? Or was God a male chauvinist after all?
Did God support the status quo, or was God a truly revolutionary being who desired freedom for all persons?

The Bible and Authority

In order to find answers to these questions, Mollenkott turned
to the Bible. This might come as a surprise to most feminists
because the common assumption among many feminists is that
the Bible is a hostile document in relation to women's rights.
Likewise, traditional Christians (especially fundamentalists)
would be surprised to find Mollenkott using the Bible as a
document in support of women's rights, for their assumption
is that the Scriptures are opposed to the equality of the sexes.
But Mollenkott has viewed the Bible quite differently from either
group. She understands the Bible as a sacred text in favor of
sexual equality. In reference to all those who hold a negative
view of the Bible in regard to women's rights, she has written:

> At the outset we must admit that Christian traditionalists and most
> radical feminists agree firmly on one point: both camps believe the
> Bible supports male supremacy in homes and churches. But while
> the traditionalists applaud biblical support for social and sexist
> hierarchy, radical feminists attack the Bible for the same reason:
> they see it as an instrument of social oppression, most notably of
> black people and women.[15]

As a result of her biblical feminism, Mollenkott has found
herself to be suspect among certain feminist groups and within
many conservative Christian churches. She is caught in the
middle. Often she will be rejected by radical feminists as a
hopeless religionist. On the other hand, traditionalist Christians
will reject her as a heretic. Indeed, the reaction she receives

from her own Christian brothers and sisters is quite confusing. In 1980 Mollenkott lamented: "At the moment it seems that I may be destined to be forever marginal: too 'radical' for most evangelicals, too 'addicted to the Bible' for many people in the main-line churches."[16]

The one thing which is certain for Mollenkott is her commitment to the Bible. In fact it was the Bible which finally confirmed her in her convictions as a champion of women's rights. "Difficult as it may be for my fundamentalist family and friends to realize," she writes, "it is precisely my study of the Bible that has radicalized me."[17] So, although she may differ with many of her feminist friends' negative attitude toward Scripture, there is no question that Mollenkott is a Christian feminist.

Mollenkott's approach to understanding Scripture is to interpret the entire Bible in light of God's revelation in Jesus Christ. Indeed, she stands within the mainstream of Christian tradition when she argues that the life and teachings of Jesus must be the ultimate measure of all biblical truth. She has written of her approach for interpreting biblical passages in daily life:

> It is my assumption that if we are interested in understanding the Christian way of relating to others [including God], the Bible must be our central source, and the teachings of Jesus must provide our major standard of judgement.[18]

In this sense, the good news of God's love and forgiveness in Jesus Christ for all people is certainly good news for women. Mollenkott will not permit this great message of God's salvation to be used as an instrument for the oppression of women or any other minority.

Jesus, Women, and Equality

In Jesus Christ we discover that God was *for* humanity, and in being *for* humanity, God was and is *for* women. This is the good news which Mollenkott discovered in her study of the Bible. From what we can gather from the New Testament stories of Jesus, it is evident that he valued women on the same par as he did men. It can even be argued that the Gospels, especially Luke, hold a special concern for the low status of women in the ancient world.

At the time of Jesus' birth, the status of women in his society was extremely low. According to the customs and laws of rabbinic Judaism, women had no status at all unless they related to men in the roles of wife and mother. In Mollenkott's words, "Only through marriage and motherhood could a woman hope to find respect or dignified status."[19] For example, the Talmud (the main body of written Jewish law) defined a woman as a "shapeless lump" before marriage who would be shaped by the husband after marriage.[20] From this perspective it was clear that religion itself served to endorse the dehumanization of women in Jesus' time.

Jesus, however, would have nothing to do with this demeaning attitude toward women. He dared to be seen in public with women even though teachers like himself (rabbis) were not supposed to appear in public with women. In addition, he defied social and religious custom by having women disciples. Although the Gospel writers do not count women disciples among the original twelve, they attested to the presence of numerous female disciples in Jesus' small band. As Mollenkott has pointed out:

> . . . remembering the prejudices of rabbinic Judaism, we can recognize how radically shocking to contemporaries was the fact that Jesus traveled with female as well as male disciples. Luke 8:1-3 tells us that as Jesus "traveled about from one city and village to another" (NIV), he was accompanied not only by the twelve, but also by *many* women.[21]

Even Jesus' male disciples were surprised at his "liberated" treatment of women. Much like men today, they were often confused and angry when one of their own sex treated women with genuine respect. This point is illustrated for us in the story of the Samaritan woman in the fourth chapter of John's Gospel. Here Jesus is found in a public conversation with a woman—a foreigner at that! When the male disciples returned from the marketplace and witnessed this situation, they were deeply upset. To make matters worse, they overheard Jesus talking theology with this woman. Theology was men's business; everybody knew that!

In this regard, Jesus' presence with women in public was a strong statement of his rejection of the social and religious customs which constrained women. His encounter with the woman who had been hemorrhaging for twelve years is another case in point. Mollenkott reminds us that in this story from Matthew 9:18-26 the woman in question "had been ritually unclean all that time (twelve years) and would have rendered unclean any man she touched."[22] Hence, her secret attempt to touch Jesus' garment in order to receive healing was done out of desperation since she could not expect to be touched by the healing hands of Jesus.

Jesus' response to this woman was more than she could have ever hoped for. After Jesus discovered who it was that had touched his garment, he declared that the woman's faith had made her well. He did not criticize her for defiling him with her touch; rather, he affirmed her faith, her person, her being! Jesus' actions assured the woman that she was acceptable even though society had defined her as "unclean." Perhaps what is most significant in this story are the actions Jesus did not take. He completely ignored the laws regarding defilement by an "unclean" woman. Rather than purify himself in a ritualistic bath, he continued his journey to the home of a local ruler and raised the ruler's daughter from the dead. As Mollenkott has stated:

> . . . he [Jesus] did not wash his clothes, bathe in water, and segregate himself until evening (Leviticus 15:27). Neither did he instruct the woman to segregate herself for seven days and then make expiation by sacrificing two pigeons at the temple (Leviticus 15:28-30). He simply proceeded on his errand of raising the ruler's daughter from the dead.[23]

In no way did Jesus accept the ritual laws which denied women their basic dignity as one of God's own.

One final example of Jesus' dealing with women clearly indicates that he rejected his society's stereotyped roles for women. In Luke 10 we have evidence that he would not accept the notion that woman's work is only in the kitchen. In this familiar story of Mary and Martha, Jesus refused to send Mary back to the kitchen when Martha complained that she was not performing her household duties. In Mollenkott's words, "When Martha complained that Mary was not helping her with the housework but rather studying the word of God at the feet of Jesus, the master refused to order Mary to play the stereotypical female role."[24] Instead, he praised Mary's sense of priorities and her commitment to learn about God's kingdom.

In all these examples we can see that Jesus affirmed the dignity and worth of women as equal heirs with men to God's blessings and promises of a new way of life—a life lived under the love and care of a merciful God. In other words, the kingdom of God which Jesus preached was inclusive of women. To be sure, the precise manner in which women and men were to relate to one another in this emerging kingdom was not spelled out in detail. However, we can only assume that the character of human relations in the new life which Jesus had to offer was consistent with his own open and caring style of life. Thus, as Mollenkott has suggested, when examining the teachings of Jesus concerning male and female relationships, we need to keep in mind the principles by which he led his own life.[25]

These principles represented a complete reversal of the world's values, especially in regard to the place of women. Jesus suggested, for example, that true greatness could be achieved in human relations by a commitment to humility and servanthood. Interestingly, these are two traits which are generally forced upon women, but in Jesus' case he is asking men and women alike voluntarily to assume these qualities. When his male disciples got into an argument about which of them would be greatest in the kingdom of heaven, Jesus made it clear that his understanding of life had little to do with the usual power games. He pointed to little children as examples of greatness. Ironically these were the very ones who had no power and no rights in their society. Much like women, children had no real status in the ancient world. But Jesus was declaring that in their weakness these little children had more power than the greatest of human beings—for such were of God's kingdom (Matthew 18:1-6).

Jesus asked his followers to submit voluntarily to one another in love. He called for mutual responsibility and accountability; this is quite different from some so-called "Christian" definitions of submission which call for women to submit while men are free to do as they please. In Jesus' view there must be equality and mutuality in submission. This kind of submission has more to do with loving than obeying. This may sound strange to the world's ears, but loving submission does not mean the enslavement of one category of people to another. In the Sermon on the Mount (Matthew 5-7), Jesus calls for all of us, men and women, to go the second mile in human relations. We are to give *freely* of ourselves without counting the cost.

As Mollenkott views the life of Jesus, she has noted a primary stress upon mutuality in love relationships. The expression of genuine love between two individuals is a two-way street in which mutual care and service are rendered one to the other. This leads to the kind of equality in relationships which insures the freedom and growth of each partner. We are indeed called to submit to one another, but we are to submit in love—a love which builds up rather than tears down. Only through this type of love can we expect to establish a lasting equality between and among the sexes. But we must remember with Mollenkott that

> . . . Christian equality is never a matter of jockeying for the dominant position. Christian equality is the result of mutual compassion, mutual concern, and mutual and voluntary loving service. The Christian way of relating achieves male-female equality through mutual submission.[26]

Jesus Christ: The God-Man?

It is hard to deny that Jesus had a positive view toward women and that his way of relating to women was "enlightened" for his times. However, the traditionalist Christian still has a fallback position in the defense of male superiority. After all, God chose to reveal "himself" in the person of a "male" named Jesus. God's choice of Jesus of Nazareth is a clear indication of the Divine preference for the male, is it not? After all, God did choose a male and not a female for "his" ultimate revelation. This is in accordance with the natural order of things! God first, male second, and female third.

This line of argument is rejected by Mollenkott as being biblically indefensible. The point of the incarnation (God's in-fleshment in Jesus Christ) is not that God became a *male*, but rather that God became a *human being*. The point is that God became flesh (*sarx*) and dwelt among us (John 1:14). As such, God was embodied in a living, breathing, full-blooded human being. The biblical stress was never upon Jesus' gender; it was upon his humanity. We speak not of Jesus' maleness; rather we speak of his humanity.

In this regard Mollenkott believes it is important for us to examine the language of the New Testament. She has observed:

> . . . when the New Testament writers refer to the incarnation of Jesus, they do not speak of his becoming *aner*, "male," but rather of his being *anthropos*, "human." Since in English the one word *man* is used to mean both "male" and "mankind" or "humanity," this important distinction is lost in English translations. That loss makes it easy to associate the Savior of the world with masculinity to the extinction of the feminine.[27]

If the real truth be known, Jesus was able to think of himself in feminine as well as masculine terms. This should be enough to dispel the notion that his maleness had theological significance. As Mollenkott reminds us, in Matthew 23:37 Jesus refers to himself as a mother hen. Here he is lamenting over Jerusalem: "O Jerusalem, Jerusalem, killing the prophets and stoning those who are sent to you! How often would I have gathered your children together as a hen gathers her brood under her wings, and you would not!"

Even more to the point, Jesus did not hesitate to identify God in feminine terms. We are well aware of the masculine images that Jesus used for the Divine, including "Father," but we often overlook an important feminine image. In the parable of the lost coin (Luke 10), Jesus clearly identifies God as a woman. In this parable God, represented by the woman householder, searches diligently until she finds the lost coin. There can be little argument about Jesus' identification of God as a woman in this parable. For verification all we need to do is look at the other two parables in Luke 10 which deal with lostness—the parable of the Good Shepherd and the parable of the Prodigal Son (better named the Forgiving Father). In all these parables of lostness, the main subject of the stories is God. In these parables Jesus provides us with rich and varied images for the Divine—God as woman householder, God as good shepherd, and God as forgiving father. As Mollenkott points out, we can no more deny God as a woman householder than we can deny God as good shepherd or forgiving father.

It would be the greatest of theological heresies to claim that Jesus' incarnation is our ultimate proof for male supremacy. As we have just seen, Jesus himself, in his view of his own nature and the nature of God, felt no compulsion to assert his masculinity or maleness. The message of the incarnation is that God became flesh because God is for humanity—men and women alike. The symbol of the incarnation must never be used as a witness for male superiority or exclusiveness. It must always remain what the biblical witness intended it to be, a recognition that God has chosen to stand with us all. Men and women inclusive!

Biblical Images of God as Female

By now it should be evident that those who follow Jesus must be prepared to open their lives to a view of God which is feminine as well as masculine. Not to do so would be to deny the life and teachings of Jesus himself. Also, should we fail to take into account the feminine face of God, we would be rejecting biblical revelation. The Bible itself supplies us with female images of God beyond the ones used by Jesus.

Before we follow Mollenkott's lead in the exploration of some of these biblical images, we need to be clear about her intent. It is not her desire to substitute a female god, a goddess, for a male god, sometimes thought of as the Lord God (Yahweh) of Scripture. In Mollenkott's way of thinking, it would be just as fallacious to argue the case for God as a female as it would be to argue that the Divine is a male. This is precisely what we would be doing if we replaced our masculine reference to God with feminine references. However, since our culture thinks almost exclusively of God in masculine images, it would be to our credit to balance this tendency with some feminine references to God. Such actions would protect us against the strong temptation to confuse God with masculinity and thereby set up an idolatry of the male.

The recovery of some of the biblical images of God as female is indeed our best safeguard against theological sexism (viewing God as only male). Mollenkott has said of the use of female imagery for God:

It might serve to remind us of the metaphoric nature of God-language if we followed the biblical practice of picturing God in feminine terms every once in a while. But it would serve no real purpose to switch completely to feminine pronouns and feminine references, because not only would we have to rewrite the Bible, but after a while we might forget all over again and begin to think of God as literally female. The big task is to achieve the balance of remembering that God's ways are not our ways, that as human beings we operate under all sorts of creaturely limitations, and that God the Creator is limited by *none* of them, including the limitations of human gender.[28]

It would not be fair, therefore, to criticize Mollenkott for wanting to make God into a woman. What she does desire to do is transform our thinking about God so that we do not fall into the easy trap of identifying God as a man.

In her book entitled *The Divine Feminine*, Mollenkott discloses over a dozen biblical images for God as female. We will look at only a few. Perhaps the most common female image for God in the Bible is a picture of God as a maternal deity. In Mollenkott's words, "Not only is the Creator depicted as carrying in the womb or birthing the creation, but also Christ and the Holy Spirit are depicted in similar roles."[29] For example, in Isaiah 42:14 we have an image of God as a mother experiencing labor pains. "For a long time I have held my peace, I have kept still and restrained myself; now I will cry out like a woman in travail, I will gasp and pant." According to Mollenkott's interpretation of this passage, we have God's anguish over the people's injustice compared to the pains of childbirth. She has written: "Powerfully, God's anguish at the human failure to embody justice is captured in the image of a woman writhing, unable to catch her breath in the pain of her travail."[30]

A different picture of God as Mother appears in Acts 17:26-28. Here Mollenkott notes that Paul portrays God as giving birth to all life. In his speech to the Athenian Council, the apostle declares that it is in God that we live, move, and have our being. This sounds like Paul has in mind a cosmic womb of some sort. As Mollenkott points out, "Although the apostle does not specifically name the womb, at no other time in human experience do we exist *within* another person."[31] What a powerful image is implied by Paul—we are all pictured as being sustained and carried by our nurturing Mother, God.

Jesus himself understood his suffering on the cross in terms of birth pangs. Through these pangs of birth a new humanity was to be born. Mollenkott has given the following interpretation to John 16:21:

> A woman, he [Jesus] said, has sorrow when her *hour is come* and her birth contractions begin, but later her sorrow is turned to joy by the actual arrival of the baby. According to John's account it was only minutes later that Jesus began to pray with the words, "Father, *the hour has come*" (17:1). What hour? The hour of Christ-the-Mother's pain and sorrow: the hour of birth pangs.[32]

This passage is an excellent example of how a biblical feminist can draw some new insights to our attention. Without violating the original intent of the Scripture being discussed, Mollenkott is able to give it a new understanding for the contemporary reader.

Another important image of God as feminine involved the biblical concept of wisdom. Often in Scriptures the feminine Hebrew term, *hokmah*, is used to represent God's wisdom. In many passages, wisdom (*hokmah*) is treated as being almost synonymous with the idea of God. Mollenkott has noted that wisdom is often equated "with the Old Testament spirit of Yahweh, and with the New Testament Holy Spirit; she is also pictured in terms that link her to Jesus the Christ, the Logos, the Word of God."[33] For example, in Proverbs 8:22, Lady Wisdom is identified as the first created being—even preceding Adam and Eve. In Colossians 1:15, we have Christ referred to as the firstborn of every creature. It appears that the connection between Christ and Lady Wisdom is no mere coincidence for the writer of Colossians!

In addition to imagining God as a mother and as Lady Wisdom, there are other feminine images: God as a mother bear, God as the female beloved, God as the bakerwoman, God as the midwife, and so on.[34] All these images are biblical. In fact, as Mollenkott suggests, there are many more feminine images for God in the Bible than we have been led to believe. That any feminine images for God have survived in the biblical texts is in itself a small miracle. Dominated by the perspective of a patriarchal society, the inspired writers of the Bible nevertheless managed to speak of God in feminine ways. Mollenkott can only attribute this to the power of the Holy Spirit. "Ordinarily," she writes, "the group in power does not depict God in terms of the group they are oppressing."[35] In this sense, it is a surprise that God of biblical times would *ever* be depicted as female— certainly the women of this period were among the oppressed. The fact that the Bible does speak of God in the feminine as well as the masculine should be a great source of hope for today's followers of Christ. As Mollenkott suggests: "The fact that this happened *rarely* should not surprise us. The fact that it happened at all *should* surprise us. And delight us. And challenge us."[36]

Is God Male or Female?

We do have a challenge before us. If we are to take the views of Virginia Mollenkott seriously, then we had best be prepared to speak of God in feminine ways. As Mollenkott has demonstrated, we do not do this in order to "prove" that God is female. This would be as wrongheaded as efforts to prove that God is male. The point is that we must correct a dangerous imbalance in our cultural and religious assumptions about the Divine. Because of our male-dominated world view we slip all too easily into the habit of speaking and acting as if God were indeed a man. For the sake of our biblical religion and for the dignity of women, we must guard against this sexist tendency.

Out of Mollenkott's life and thought we have gleaned several important insights concerning the relation of women of faith to our patriarchal society and religion. First of all, we have learned that our theological perspective needs to be inclusive rather than exclusive if we are to honor and respect the involvement of both sexes in God's emerging kingdom. The painful experiences of exclusion which Mollenkott faced within her own life must be rejected as a pattern for our Christian way of life. Prejudice, narrow-minded theologies, and relationships defined by male superiority have no credibility for those who seek truly to follow Christ.

Second, we have learned from Mollenkott the importance of maintaining the Bible and Jesus Christ as sources for authority

MOLLENKOTT: Is God Male or Female?

in evaluating the true nature of God and human relationships. It is most helpful to remember that even Scripture must be judged according to the life and teachings of Jesus. Christians can never go too far astray in understanding God's will if they remain fixed upon Jesus Christ as the norm for assessing truth. In the matter of how men and women should relate, we have discovered that with Jesus the primary consideration can be defined as a loving submission of one to another. This kind of submission has equality and mutuality as its hallmarks.

Third, Mollenkott teaches us about the necessity of being opened up to the full implications of the Christian gospel. We must be willing to recognize that God's Good News is good news for us all. It is especially good news for those who have been suppressed. And it is time that we recognize that women as a category of people have indeed experienced life as suppressive. The church needs to become more inclusive in its God-language. In its worship and devotion it needs to use feminine as well as masculine images for God. This, in itself, will not turn around a sexist society, but it will be a clear signal of the church's support for equality among the sexes.

Thanks to Virginia Mollenkott and other biblical feminists, we are in a position to open the church to a new day. Certainly, there is much to be done in the ongoing work of interpreting Scripture. For example, Mollenkott and others have reconsidered Paul's work in the New Testament in an effort to determine whether it deserves the condemnation it has received from many feminists. Above all, honesty is required as we examine our own religious traditions in relation to issues of sexism. We have to examine our own hearts, and we need to pray to God, our Mother and our Father, for a new church and a new society— one which is free of gender discrimination.

Actually, if we are willing to dare, we can break down the stereotypical views of God as male. If we dare, we can truly open our Christian communities to full participation by women at every level—including leadership and the ordained ministry. Men, as well as women, in the church are called to become biblical feminists so that this can happen. The challenge is clearly before us; the question is before us. Is God male or female? If

88 WITNESSES BEFORE DAWN

we answer that God cannot ultimately be considered either one
or the other, then we must be prepared to stop acting as if "he"
is a male!

Recommended Readings

Virginia Mollenkott

The Divine Feminine: The Biblical Imagery of God as Female. New
York: The Crossroad Publishing Co., 1983.
Speech, Silence, Action! Nashville, Abingdon Press, 1980.
Women, Men and the Bible. Nashville: Abingdon Press, 1977.

NOTES

[1] Virginia Ramey Mollenkott, *Speech, Silence, Action!* (Nashville: Abingdon Press,
1980), pp. 44-45.
[2] *Ibid.*, p. 41.
[3] *Ibid.*, p. 42.
[4] *Ibid.*, p. 46.
[5] *Ibid.*, p. 22.
[6] *Ibid.*, p. 27.
[7] *Ibid.*, p. 23.
[8] For an elaboration on the theme of Christian humanism, it is helpful to refer
to one of Mollenkott's earlier works entitled *Adamant and Stone-Chips: A Christian
Humanist Approach to Knowledge,* published by Word Books in 1967.
[9] Virginia Ramey Mollenkott, *Speech, Silence, Action!* p. 20.
[10] *Ibid.*, p. 39.
[11] *Ibid.*, p. 18.
[12] *Ibid.*, p. 20.
[13] *Ibid.*
[14] *Ibid.*, p. 21.
[15] Virginia Ramey Mollenkott, *Women, Men, and the Bible* (Nashville: Abingdon
Press, 1977), p. 90.
[16] Virginia Ramey Mollenkott, *Speech, Silence, Action!*, p. 25.
[17] *Ibid.*, pp. 25-26.
[18] Virginia Ramey Mollenkott, *Women, Men, and the Bible,* p. 9.
[19] *Ibid.*, p. 12.
[20] *Ibid.*
[21] *Ibid.*, p. 19.
[22] *Ibid.*, p. 13.
[23] *Ibid.*, p. 14.
[24] *Ibid.*, p. 18.
[25] *Ibid.*, p. 10.
[26] *Ibid.*, p. 33.
[27] *Ibid.*, p. 61.
[28] *Ibid.*, p. 68.
[29] Virgina Ramey Mollenkott, *The Divine Feminine: The Biblical Imagery of God as
Female* (New York: The Crossroad Publishing Co., 1983), p. 15. Copyright ©
1983 by the author. Reprinted by permission of The Crossroad Publishing Company.

[30] *Ibid.*

[31] *Ibid.*, p. 16.

[32] *Ibid.*, p. 17.

[33] *Ibid.*, p. 100.

[34] Mollenkott's *The Divine Feminine* should be pursued by those who would like to develop a better working knowledge of the various feminine images for God as female in the Bible.

[35] Virginia Ramey Mollenkott, *The Divine Feminine*, p. 112.

[36] *Ibid.*

5

ELIZABETH O'CONNOR:
How Do We Build Community?

> So then you are no longer strangers and sojourners, but you are fellow citizens with the saints and members of the household of God, built upon the foundation of the apostles and prophets, Christ Jesus himself being the cornerstone, in whom the whole structure is joined together and grows into a holy temple in the Lord; in whom you also are built into it for a dwelling place of God in the Spirit.
>
> —Ephesians 2:19-22

How do we build community? In what ways can we become a "household of God" committed to Jesus Christ and the kingdom he preached and demonstrated? How do we "strangers" and "sojourners" become fellow citizens with the apostles and the prophets as the writer of Ephesians has suggested? Can we find communities of faith in today's world who are committed to Jesus Christ as the cornerstone of life? These questions have always been important for those who bear the name of Christ. In fact, questions of this nature are being asked by many churches in America today. Many of us want to know about "community" because we sense that it is missing from our Christian experience.

The creation of community in the name of Jesus Christ may indeed be the most difficult, and the most challenging, aspect of contemporary Christian living. The problem is not that we lack literature and critical reflection on this important topic. Church shelves are filled with pamphlets and books dedicated to the exploration of the meaning of Christian community. We have many theological definitions of the Christian community, and we have numerous consultants available to advise us in the area of church growth. Yet we are without purposeful vision. What we are really looking for are living models of Christian communities—communities that are alive!

The Church of the Saviour in Washington, D.C., is one such community. It has been committed to the task of building community for over three decades. Under the leadership of its pastor, Gordon Cosby, this church has held to the gospel of Jesus Christ without becoming "traditionalist" and it has achieved social relevancy without becoming "faddish." The primary interpreter of the life of this church has been one of its staff members, Elizabeth O'Connor. Her own life question of how to build Christian community has placed her in a strategic position to write about this fellowship which is dedicated precisely to that task. By becoming acquainted with Elizabeth O'Connor's life and thought, we will be placed in an excellent position to identify key elements for the building of a Christian community in today's church and today's world.

Finding and Celebrating a Common Life

Elizabeth O'Connor grew up in a family in which there was an absence of community. She was raised in a New York City household filled with turmoil. The frenzied activities of her parents made it difficult for young Elizabeth to find either peace or quiet; she struggled to carve out her own space in a chaotic home life. During her childhood the Great Depression caused an inordinate amount of attention to be given to financial matters. Every event in the O'Connor home sooner or later became a monetary crisis.

O'Connor recalls that a tremendous amount of her time was dedicated to dealing with "adult problems." She has written: "In the close circle of my peers we all seemed busy trying to parent the needy grown-ups with whom we lived."[1] Coming to the aid of adults was emotionally draining, and it robbed Elizabeth of the time necessary for her own growth and development. Looking back over this period, she has confessed, "Only much later did we learn that in trying to be parents we missed growing up ourselves."[2] This was not a happy childhood. The playfulness which releases children to be relaxed in the process of growth was conspicuously absent.

Religion was not a major factor in Elizabeth O'Connor's early development. Although she had a natural curiosity about the spiritual dimension of life, her father did not permit formal expression of religion within his household. As a disillusioned Roman Catholic he had no use for organized religion. He claimed that the church's primary reason for existing was to "rob the poor of their money."[3] As a consequence of her father's antagonism toward the Catholic church, O'Connor received no religious instruction during her youth. Her only exposure to Christianity came from the gentle Catholic piety of her grandmother.

When Elizabeth O'Connor was introduced to the Church of the Saviour as a young woman, she had almost no idea of what to expect from a Christian fellowship. She had agreed to attend worship at this Washington congregation because a friend insisted that she accompany her to the church. At the time, O'Connor was working for a New York advertising firm. The year was 1953 and Gordon Cosby, the founding minister of the Church of the Saviour, had gained national attention for developing a Christian congregation of renewal in Washington's inner city. However, Elizabeth O'Connor had no interest in all of this church business!

Indeed, she was woefully unprepared for what she experienced at the Church of the Saviour. She did not understand the peculiar language of the church. She remembers knowing so little about church life that when the congregation sang "blest be the tie that binds," she thought they were singing "blest be the tithe that binds." O'Connor can recall making the comment to friends that the people at the Church of the Saviour took their tithing so seriously that they sang about it every Sunday!

She was nevertheless strangely drawn to the people of this congregation. Something brought her back to the church again and again. For the first time in her life she had discovered a group of people who knew how to celebrate a common life together. People at the Church of the Saviour were serious about their worship and they worked together for the improvement of their own lives and the life of the community surrounding the church. Elizabeth O'Connor knew that there was something here that she wanted; and even though she made it a rule never to sign guest books, she signed the register of the church after her very first visit. She understood that something very significant was happening in her life and she wanted to record the moment for posterity.[4]

To become a member of the Church of the Saviour, O'Connor learned that she must embark on a double journey. Each member was called to an inward and an outward journey. Individuals were asked to examine their interior lives in light of the gospel message. In practical terms this meant that each member needed to be open to the exploration of his or her own spiritual life. Study and prayer were emphasized as ways to locate the crucial issues to be addressed for the purpose of personal renewal in Christ. Each person in preparation for membership had to complete a rigorous series of courses in the church's "School of Christian Living."

In commitment to an outward journey of discipleship, every member of the church was asked to belong to a mission group. With fewer than two hundred members, the Church of the Saviour has established an unbelievable number of effective missions over the past several decades. These groups, made up of seven to twelve individuals, have created programs for the aging in their community; they have renovated apartment buildings for low-income occupancy in their inner-city area; they have developed programs for the care of neglected and abandoned children; they have established polycultural education programs for the neighborhood; they have provided leadership training for ghetto youth; they have created an inner-city coffeehouse; they have provided for a medical clinic for the poor; and the list goes on!

In fact, the ministries of these small mission groups have been so effective that they have caused the Church of the Saviour to divide into six separate Christian communities. Since 1976 the Church of the Saviour has really been a half dozen different churches, each with its own leadership, worship, training for discipleship, administrative council and budget.[5] This, then, is the kind of dynamic Christian community to which Elizabeth O'Connor has been dedicated for three decades. Today she can still be found at her own mission station—the Potter's House, an inner-city coffeehouse.

Creating Community

Elizabeth O'Connor is convinced that the only way to build community is to build community. In other words, community cannot be discussed for very long in the abstract. It must be given visible expression. Even as O'Connor writes about how to build community, she reflects a hard-core realism. Her description of "community" involves both theological and psychological insights, but she recognizes that what she truly knows about community she has learned from personal involvement in her church.
She writes:

> I am neither theologian nor psychiatrist and I cannot add to the literature that has been written on the subject of religion and psychiatry. I can write only as a member of a congregation who can speak experientially of what is often only written of in the abstract.[6]

Since 1961 the Potter's House has been Elizabeth O'Connor's concrete expression of community. This storefront coffeehouse located at 1658 Columbia Road in our nation's capital functions as a "gift-evoking" and a "gift-bearing" community for all those who enter its doors.[7] An identification and use of the gifts which God has given each of us marks a major thrust of the coffeehouse's mission. This urban cafe is a nurturing and caring type of place. There is something quite distinct about its atmosphere; it can be filled with people and yet be very quiet and peaceful. It is a place where the climate is right for intimate conversation and the sharing of life in significant ways.

Prior to my visit to the Potter's House in the fall of 1982, I had studied Elizabeth O'Connor's ideas about cultivating the gifts which God has given us. Now at the coffeehouse I could see how this worked. When I arrived at the Potter's House, I was taken to an out-of-the-way table where Ms. O'Connor and a friend were involved in conversation. I soon learned that Elizabeth's friend, like myself, had come from a distant place. It is not unusual for many of the Potter's House "drop-ins" to be distant travelers on a pilgrimage looking for "community." This particular friend was from Chicago, and she had come to Washington as a volunteer to help the Church of the Saviour with its newly established free employment agency for the neighborhood unemployed. She explained to me that she was a director of an upper echelon employment service in Chicago, but that she had lost interest in her work because it did not seem to count for much. Somehow she was befriended by Elizabeth O'Connor, and now she found herself using her management talents to organize the Church of the Saviour's free employment agency. She had discovered new life in this mission and it was written all over her face. Elizabeth had been able to evoke from her friend gifts and talents which could be used in service of those in need. That is the way things work around the Potter's House. This is community in action!

Another woman I met at the Potter's House was also being encouraged to develop her gifts for the benefit of others. She arrived at our table carrying a large paper bag filled with carpet samples; she was the wife of a top aide to a U.S. senator. Earlier in the week the old, gray stone Victorian house which serves as the headquarters for the Church of the Saviour had been fire-bombed by an arsonist. Elizabeth O'Connor's office had to be rebuilt and redecorated. The senatorial aide's wife had been given the task of redecorating the burned-out office.

I was fascinated with how Elizabeth cultivated her friend's latent gifts. Realizing that her friend desired to explore her talents as an interior decorator, she had given her the assignment of renovating her office interior. Once again I was witness to the "gift-evoking" and "gift-bearing" ministry which exemplified the community spirit of the Church of the Saviour. Within the span of an hour's time I had experienced firsthand what Elizabeth O'Connor had said was so difficult to write about in the abstract—namely, a genuine sense of community.[8]

Journey Inward, Journey Outward

Elizabeth O'Connor and the people of the Church of the Saviour believe that community cannot be created unless each member of the community is committed to personal renewal. All those who participate in the life of the church must be willing to take the journey inward and the journey outward. The inward journey involves serious self-examination, the exploration of strengths and weaknesses, an evaluation of gifts and talents, and a readiness to change. The outward journey is an extension of the inward journey; it represents a commitment to mission and it is directed by the gifts and talents discovered during the inward journey.

In her accounts about the life of the Church of the Saviour, Elizabeth O'Connor has pieced together her church's understanding of how personal renewal leads to community formation. In the first chapter of *Journey Inward, Journey Outward*, she explains what her book is about, and by implication, she reveals the agenda of the Church of the Saviour.

> This is a book about the "narrow gate," which will henceforth be referred to as the inward journey. It is a book concerned with the renewal of the church, for it holds that renewal cannot come to the church unless its people are on an inward journey. It holds with equal emphasis that renewal cannot come to the church unless its people are on an outward journey.[9]

According to O'Connor, there are only two directions for our lives—we can take either the wide road or the narrow road. "The wide road," she writes, "might be called the way of unconsciousness and the narrow road the way of consciouness."[10]

The Church of the Saviour views its task as enabling its members to gain a confident awareness of their inward and outward journeys. The way to the narrow road is not easy. The "narrow gate" stands before us as Jesus said (Matthew 7:13-14). It leads to life—the fullness of life which includes community. However, the choice to accept conscious responsibility for our journeys requires commitment. It also requires risk, openness to change, and endurance of the pain which usually accompanies significant growth. Elizabeth O'Connor has said of this journey along the narrow road: "One, it leads to life, but Two, it is a hard way, and Three, few find it."[11] The Church of the Saviour's invitation to its membership to take the narrow road comes with the complete recognition that there are no shortcuts on this spiritual pilgrimage. The journey begins with the self, but it

ends in community. It starts with an inward examination, yet it
ends with an outward ministry to others.

Beginning with the Self

In Elizabeth O'Connor's estimate there are three different
kinds of encounters along the path of our inward and outward
journeys, and each of these ultimately leads to the formation of
community. The first of these engagements involves the discovery of our own true selves. In this engagement, we are asked
to deal with the unexamined ambiguities which reside at the
core of our lives. We are invited to serious self-examination. In
the language of the Bible we are asked to confront our true
nature, that is, our sinful selves.

Engaging our sinful selves is not easy. Many of us have developed a convenient catalogue of "sins" which we confess from
time to time, but this is only a spiritual smoke screen. We are
adept at revealing those parts of ourselves which we feel comfortable about disclosing, our little "sins." However, the Bible
mandates that we confront those inner aspects of ourselves
which are most painful for us to face. We are challenged to
identify those things which are a source of our self-alienation.
In other words, we are asked to wrestle with our own "demons."

Elizabeth O'Connor notes that the so-called "sins" which we
are so quick to confess are nothing more than window-dressing
for a shallow spirituality. However, the biblical notion of sin has
nothing to do with our pious list of wrongdoings. Sin, in the
biblical sense, is rooted in our alienated human condition. This,
then, results in our "sinful" activities, but sin itself is a state of
alienation which goes much deeper than our so-called "sinful"
actions. For example, in the Genesis story of Adam and Eve,
the "original sin" involves an attitude of pride which results in
disobedient action. Eating the forbidden fruit is Adam and Eve's
downfall, but the *real* sin had already occurred. Adam and Eve
had chosen to alienate themselves from their Creator, and in
the process they alienated themselves from each other. The game
of blaming others for our sinful state had begun. Adam blamed
Eve and Eve blamed the serpent!

Our human situation has always been one of separation and

estrangement from God. This condition, which is illustrated for us throughout the Bible and in our own experience, has placed us in a difficult position. We realize that we are not in communion with the Creator; there is even a sense of disharmony *within* the human spirit itself. Nothing can seem to heal our deep sense of alienation! We have been alienated for so long that we do not expect reconciliation.

However, Elizabeth O'Connor argues that we need not settle for our alienated condition, as if it were normative. We can plunge beneath the surface of our lives, and we can dare to confront the sinful (alienated) condition of our souls. She has written:

> As people on an inward journey we are committed to growing in consciousness, to becoming people in touch with our real selves, so that we know not only what flows at the surface, but what goes on in the depths of us. [12]

This deeper look at ourselves requires that we deal with our darker and more sinful side. Yet it is only in this confrontation that we can assure interaction with all parts of ourselves, even the parts we would rather ignore.

O'Connor is able to make this same point about self-alienation through the language of modern psychology. For example, she finds Carl Jung's use of the concept of our "shadow side" to be very helpful in the description of our human predicament. Through the "shadow side" Jung introduces us to the enemy within. Along with the light which is in our lives, we also have the darkness, and it also belongs to us. We must be prepared to claim our "shadow side" if we desire to be renewed within our own spirits.

The idea that we have darkness within us does not fit well into many modern perspectives. We have difficulty accepting the idea that our moral and spiritual character contains darkness as well as light. We find it hard to admit that the evil we confront often comes from within. Moral perfectionists often view evil as coming from the outside; it is said to be external to the self. We are like the unfaithful marital partner who blames external circumstances for the breakup of a marriage, but who seldom admits to being a part of the problem. We can identify evil in others, yet we cannot see it in ourselves. According to Elizabeth O'Connor, people who consistently locate the "enemy" outside of themselves are people who have not seriously embarked upon an inward journey.

The "shadow side" for all its importance, however, is only one of the many aspects of the self which we engage on the journey inward. In her book *Our Many Selves,* O'Connor speaks of numerous "selves" which contend for our allegiance. She became aware of her many "selves" while passing through a period of tremendous personal struggle. She recalls: "It was during a time of painful conflict that I first began to experience myself as more than one. It was as though I sat in the midst of many selves."[13] During this period of her life, the story of the Gerasene demoniac in Luke's Gospel became a parable of her own personal situation. In the demoniac, she envisioned a poor soul, like herself, who was possessed by demons. Their name was "Legion" because there were so many of them (Luke 8:26-39).

For Elizabeth O'Connor the Gerasene demoniac was the story of many modern men and women. Each time we stand at a crossroads in life we are confronted by a "multiplicity of selves" each telling us what to do next. Indeed, *we* are Legion. When we seek to make important decisions, we hear the many voices within ourselves. Each voice, or self, has a different opinion. We hear from our positive self (the light) and we hear from our negative self (the dark). We also hear from our ambiguous self; this is when we are especially unclear as to what to do next. We find our "person" divided in an argument against itself. Using Freud's categories, we encounter the "multiplicity of selves" as id, ego, and superego. Borrowing from the psychology of transactional analysis, we find ourselves playing the tapes of the parent, the child, and the adult within us. Regardless of our tools of analysis, the fact remains that we are divided against ourselves.

Another self which we often ignore is the suffering self. Elizabeth O'Connor encourages us to recognize this aspect of our personality. She believes we have created a false mythology about suffering. The myth lies in the assumption that we can escape suffering. We often construct our own private religion as a buffer against suffering. This, however, can be a great barrier to personal wholeness. Unless we face our own suffering and develop a sensitivity to the suffering of others, we will never know personal or social fulfillment.

O'Connor contends that we must recognize the reality of suffering in order to learn from it. Her intent is not to give positive meaning to suffering. There is no virtue in glorifying suffering. However, O'Connor does want to know what it is we might learn from suffering since it is so much a part of our human existence. She notes that those who suffer physical pain often become more aware of the "important" things in life as a result of their pain. In ministering to others who suffer we too can learn from suffering. The biblical admonition to visit the sick is a call for us to learn from, as well as to serve, the afflicted. We can learn from suffering if we have the courage to claim it as a part of our own being, as one of our many selves. Or as Elizabeth O'Connor has written: "Perhaps if we kept more fully our own desert watches—stayed longer where the pain is—we would be different when we left the wilderness."[14]

One last point needs to be made about the engagement of the self. It is a journey that can turn sour. Introspection is healthy, but only as long as it remains open-ended. Total preoccupation with the self can be the worst form of idolatry. We are in constant danger of worshiping the self. Unfortunately, some people make their quests to "know" themselves a lifetime vocation. The only safeguard against this kind of narcissism is the recognition that our true self cannot emerge until we are willing to transcend ourselves.

Elizabeth O'Connor likes to point to the works of Christian saints as a way of affirming the step beyond self-engagement. For example, the great Augustine's *Confessions* are saved from being the most blatant form of self-idolatry because in the end Augustine can point beyond himself to God. This saint of late antiquity was unwilling to rest until he found his rest in his Creator. This is precisely O'Connor's point. A willingness to keep the engagement of self open for the engagement of God preserves the dynamism and vitality of our journey inward.

Encountering God

A second type of engagement which ultimately leads to community is engagement with God. Elizabeth O'Connor is convinced that our spiritual pilgrimages cannot bypass the divine encounter. We need more than a theology about God, we need to engage the living God. There is a difference. Just as we must be willing to explore our inner selves in depth, we must also look deep within our own lives for God's presence.

In the Church of the Saviour's School of Christian Living, students are encouraged to study Christian tradition for help in understanding their own encounters with God. They are invited to practice the ancient disciplines of prayer and meditation. Elizabeth O'Connor states the philosophy of her church in the following way:

> The person on the inward journey in the church come-of-age will be familiar with all forms of prayer from a simple petition and intercession to meditation and contemplation and the prayer of silence. He will take time to experience a life that is different from his life, and to see a world that is not visible to the ordinary glance.[15]

This advocacy for an experience of things "not visible to the ordinary glance" is not meant as a traditionalist plea for an adoption of antiquated spiritual disciplines. The emphasis here is upon the believer's contemporary involvement in the ongoing life of the living God.

Members of the Church of the Saviour are called to view life in a revolutionary way; they are asked to be aware of God's presence in today's world. Prayer can help this awareness as can the study of the Bible. In this regard, each member of the Church of the Saviour is required to be involved in a regular program of Bible study. Members are encouraged to study the men and women of biblical faith until they locate themselves within the struggles of these ancient stories. They are encouraged to meditate upon the biblical God until that God becomes the living Lord of their own lives. In this sense, reading the Scriptures becomes a contemporary discipline. The Bible becomes a living document in which God can be encountered again and again, ever new and ever fresh.

The development of spiritual disciplines is foundational for the Church of the Saviour in its preparation for mission. Since the church's goal is to discover what God is doing in our world, the inner life must be kept alive so that the outer life can serve. Elizabeth O'Connor counsels members not to dwell too long on spiritual disciplines which are not challenging. We should avoid things which are overly familiar. The familiar can become a roadblock to the discovery of God's actions. Therefore, the person who has done quiet, meditative readings is encouraged to try a more active type of meditation. The individual who likes music as a discipline of the spirit is challenged to practice the discipline of silence. In short, there are needs for freshness, challenge, and risk-taking in our engagement with God.

Elizabeth O'Connor believes that our age needs to rediscover the same type of enthusiasm for the experience of God as we have for the experience of self. Psychology is the language of our culture; it is time to reaffirm the language of spirituality. In the process we need to recognize that our renewed search for God is undergirded by God's continued search for us. According to the Bible, God has been in relentless pursuit of the human race from the very beginning. God has not given up on us and this makes the renewal of our lives a real possibility. In Elizabeth O'Connor's words:

It is change that we must struggle for, but when it comes it is always by the grace of God. It is His Spirit that broods over the void and darkness of our lives, and over the face of the abyss in us. It is God who says, "Let there be light." It is God who sends a Son that by the power of the Resurrection what is unknown in us may be lifted up and made known.[16]

Engaging Others

The third and final kind of engagement we encounter on our journey is the engagement of others. Actually, the engagement of others brings to completeness our quest for community. Elizabeth O'Connor has written that engaging others ". . . is bound up with the whole concept of the church."[17] As Christians we are called to engage one another in the name of Jesus Christ. Those who bear the name of Christ are called to view relationships in a Christological way. Jesus Christ, for the follower, becomes the paradigm for all relationships—especially those within the church.

In the case of the Church of the Saviour, people "belong" because they have confessed Jesus Christ as Lord. The lordship of Christ is the bond which shapes the fellowship. Without a recognition of this bond, fellowship cannot exist and ministry cannot be carried out. Elizabeth O'Connor insists that commitment to Jesus Christ forms the only true basis for church membership: "A person is not received into the membership of the church because he is a certain type or because he has arrived at a certain place in life, but because he can say Christ is Lord."[18]

Within the fellowship of the Church of the Saviour, this personal affirmation of Christ's lordship is accompanied by a public commitment to one of the missions of the church. The moment we say yes to Jesus Christ, the Church of the Saviour believes we also say yes to the mission and ministry of Jesus Christ, and this mission and ministry cannot be carried out without some form of Christian community. There is no such thing as a solitary Christian. By definition, Christians must be "in Christ" and thereby in fellowship with others for the sake of Christian discipleship within the world.

This means that Christians must learn how to get along with one another even when they do not like one another. It is said that we choose our friends but not our families, and the same can be said for our spiritual family, the church. Like the disciples of the New Testament we are called together by Jesus Christ, but also like the disciples we do not choose our brothers and sisters in the faith. We do not have the luxury (thank God!) of choosing who else is to join us in the work of Christ. Elizabeth O'Connor has put it this way: "Christ does the calling, and this is very threatening if we belong to his Church, because the people he calls are the people with whom we are to have intimate belonging."[19] The theological fact is that we are called to share life together in intimate ways with people we might not choose as friends under other circumstances.

Is it any wonder then that the majority of our churches opt not to take the call to community all that seriously? The amount of work it takes to deal honestly and openly with one another as brothers and sisters in Christ is staggering. Being a community in Christ requires a tremendous amount of time and energy. Therefore, in most of our churches we are not asked to engage one another in the name of Jesus Christ; mostly what is required of us is the maintenance of superficial relationships in noncontroversial settings. But what if the church took itself seriously? What if its members invested their time and resources into the church the way they do into their families and vocations? This is precisely what the Church of the Saviour has attempted.

The church believes that simply "keeping the lid on" by avoiding controversy is not being true to the spirit of Christ. After all, families cannot grow in significant ways if everyone handles everyone else with kid gloves. It is the same with the church; there must be serious engagement within the fellowship for the sake of the fellowship. Elizabeth O'Connor was very close to the truth when she pondered the question as to why there is so little community in the church today:

> My guess is that we have so little real community in our churches because we have chosen to keep life on a polite, superficial plane rather than suffer the agony of coping with the problems that arise when we commit ourselves to any close covenant relationship.[20]

The only way to guard against this kind of superficiality in the church is to commit ourselves to the biblical concept of covenant. A covenant is a binding agreement between two parties. In the case of the church, it is a theological binder which holds together the people and their God. The covenant only has strength, however, if commitment is found among the membership.

For the Church of the Saviour, this means a commitment to stay together despite all forms of internal conflicts and confrontations which they know the members will pass through in Jesus' name. Elizabeth O'Connor notes that the commitment to stay together has a liberating quality. It allows the church to endure controversy without the constant pressure of solving internal disputes on the spot. Because of the covenant, the church knows that it will not collapse the next time brother "A" and sister "B" are in an argument. With this kind of working covenant, the members do not need to place tight bandages on wounds which should be allowed to heal in the open air. According to O'Con-

nor: "We can take the risk of telling a brother what stands
between us, if we know there will be another time when we are
together, and it does not depend on what does or does not
happen in this moment."[21]

The commitment to stay together in a covenant relationship
makes the possibility for building community real. Perhaps the
greatest gift evident in the Church of the Saviour is its ability
to cultivate such commitment on the part of its members. Most
of us have had little experience with this kind of community
commitment. Staying together for the sake of Jesus Christ and
each other is a radical notion. It is even more radical when the
commitment to mission is present. Without question, among
the members of the Church of the Saviour, Christian community
has absolute priority and primacy in the Christian life. Elizabeth
O'Connor brings home the radical nature of this kind of commitment in her book *Call to Commitment*:

> This means that we do not leave because we have wanderlust or
> need a change, or because the job opportunities are better in an-
> other city, or because the demands are too great, or because things
> have not turned out as we hoped.[22]

The journey toward community stands or falls on the issue
of commitment. This commitment comes in the form of a renewal
of the self and a dedicated quest for God, but in its fullness it
must also include a commitment to community. It is Elizabeth
O'Connor's contention that the church of Jesus Christ must bear
a continuous witness to the possibility of genuine community—
a community in which the members honestly and openly engage
one another for the sake of Christ's ministry in the world.

How Do We Build Community?

What we have learned about community from the theological
perspective of Elizabeth O'Connor and the Church of the Saviour
is that community formation in the name of Jesus Christ is
focused upon the quality of relationships. Community cannot
come about in our fellowships unless we take the time necessary
to nurture each other's gifts. We need to pay far more attention
to how it is we might evoke gifts from one another. We also
need to be a gift-bearing fellowship. Like Elizabeth O'Connor,

we need to explore ways in which our personal talents can be used in the service of others.

In addition to the stress on quality relationships in which we identify and celebrate our gifts, the Christian fellowship must encourage its members to travel through the narrow gate. We need to risk the difficult journey inward and outward so that our whole life can be renewed. Along the way we need to be conscious of the threefold engagement of self, God, and others. During our pilgrimage we must also recognize that as Christians we travel with Christ as our companion. When we travel from self to God to community and back again, we are well advised to remember that for the Christian it is Christ who must be visible every step along the way.

Finally, with Elizabeth O'Connor, we should understand that the building of Christian community cannot be done piecemeal. It requires that the whole person be developed—in terms of both our inward and outward journeys. Being in community ultimately means moving toward completion as sons and daughters of God. It is only in community that we learn the meaning of our full humanity and, for Christians, our fullness as a new creation in Christ. It is not that we lose our individuality for the sake of a corporate identity in the community. Elizabeth O'Connor's own personality is a testament against that misconceived notion. It is rather that in community we have the potential of becoming all we were intended to be, both from the perspective of our personal development and our social responsibility. It may very well be that the creation of a new sense of community in our time will spark the renewal of Christian commitment in our generation. One thing is certain: Without a renewal of Christian community we will not find our way to faithful service in Christ for the sake of the world.

Recommended Readings

Elizabeth O'Connor

Call to Commitment. New York: Harper & Row, Publishers, Inc., 1963.

Eighth Day of Creation. Waco, Texas: Word Books, 1971.

Journey Inward, Journey Outward. New York: Harper & Row, Publishers, Inc., 1968.

Our Many Selves. New York: Harper & Row, Publishers, Inc., 1971.

NOTES

[1] Elizabeth O'Connor, *Letters to Scattered Pilgrims* (New York: Harper & Row, Publishers, Inc., 1979), p. 132.

[2] *Ibid.*

[3] Notes from a personal interview with Elizabeth O'Connor in November, 1982.

[4] Personal interview, November, 1982.

[5] O'Connor, *Letters to Scattered Pilgrims*, p. xiv.

[6] Elizabeth O'Connor, *Journey Inward, Journey Outward* (New York: Harper & Row, Publishers, Inc., 1968), p. 53.

[7] Elizabeth O'Connor, *Eighth Day of Creation* (Waco, Texas: Word Books, 1971), p. 8.

[8] A more complete discussion of "gift-evoking" and "gift-bearing" can be found in *Our Many Selves* and in *Journey Inward, Journey Outward*, chapter 3, "Calling Forth of Gifts."

[9] O'Connor, *Journey Inward, Journey Outward*, p. 9.

[10] *Ibid.*, p. 5.

[11] *Ibid.*, p. 8.

[12] *Ibid.*, p. 13.

[13] Elizabeth O'Connor, *Our Many Selves* (New York: Harper & Row, Publishers, Inc., 1971), p. 3.

[14] *Ibid.*, p. 96.

[15] O'Connor, *Journey Inward, Journey Outward*, p. 19.

[16] O'Connor, *Our Many Selves*, p. 59.

[17] O'Connor, *Journey Inward, Journey Outward*, p. 24.

[18] *Ibid.*

[19] *Ibid.*

[20] O'Connor, *Eighth Day of Creation*, p. 35.

[21] O'Connor, *Journey Inward, Journey Outward*, p. 25.

[22] O'Connor, *Call to Commitment* (New York: Harper & Row, Publishers, Inc., 1963), p. 40.

6

DOM HELDER CAMARA:
How Can We Do Justice?

He has showed you, O man, what is good;
and what does the LORD require of you but
to do justice and to love kindness,
and to walk humbly with your God?
—Micah 6:8

How can we do justice? This
question has been a central part of our religious tradition since
the days of the Old Testament prophets. Can we as Christians
champion the cause of social justice in our times? Do we have
the courage of Jesus to stand with the poor, the oppressed, and
the socially disfranchised? These are controversial issues, and
always will be, but the truth is that more and more contemporary
people of faith are getting involved in matters of justice.

Today, as in every age, there are prophetic witnesses who can
point the way toward just action. God has not left us without
our prophets, and one of the most instructive of these prophets
is a Brazilian named Dom Helder Camara. Since 1964 he has
been the archbishop of the Roman Catholic Church in Recife
and Olinda, Brazil. He is known as the bishop to "the poorest
of the poor." His episcopal area in Brazil's northeast region
represents the poorest and most densely populated land in Latin
America. The vast majority of his religious flock lives in abject
poverty, and the life expectancy is a meager thirty-five years.
The millions of peasants who reside in Dom Helder's jurisdiction
have little or no hope for the future. Their lives are held in

economic bondage by wealthy landowners who oppose all forms of social change.

In this setting Dom Helder has raised the cry for social justice. He has become a voice for the poor of his land. He speaks for those who have no voice in Brazil, and as a matter of principle he speaks for all those around the world who are victims of social and economic injustice. In so doing, he has raised radical questions of faith and value. He wants to know about our attitude toward the poor of this earth.

> Do the shacks in which they live deserve the name of house? Is what they eat nourishment? Are the rags they wear clothes? Can the situation in which they vegetate, without health, without expectations, without vision, without ideals be called life? . . . Christianity is not content with your alms—it demands from you justice for your workers. . . .

> Why is the Church getting involved in these questions which are economic rather than spiritual? . . . These are human problems and the human person is one and indivisible; it is the moral law which is violated when the fundamental rights of the person are threatened or ignored. . . .[1]

Dom Helder speaks these words to us as a prophet from a foreign land. His native tongue, Portuguese, is not our language. His cultural customs are quite different from ours. Most of us do not share in his religious tradition of Latin American Catholicism. However, his words and actions have global significance. We can learn much from Dom Helder Camara about how to do justice in our age.

A Journey Toward Seeking Justice

Dom Helder was born into a poor Brazilian family at Fortaleza in 1909. His father was a bookkeeper and a part-time journalist who was a Masonic freethinker. Although he had little use for the Catholic church, he saw to it that his children were baptized and presented for confirmation. Dom Helder's mother was a grade school teacher who taught students in a rented schoolhouse which also served as the Camara home. Six of her children died in early childhood, five of them of dysentery during a one-month period. She waited, helpless, for medical supplies which never arrived. Dom Helder has said that he can remember the poverty his family had to endure. This had a profound effect on his decision to enter the priesthood. In a recent interview, he reported, ". . . I cannot help but remember that I myself knew hunger and misery; that I saw my mother weep and my father fall silent from bitterness when there was nothing to eat, when there was not enough bread among their children."[2]

By the age of eight Dom Helder was convinced that he wanted to become a priest. He wanted to commit his life to helping others; he wanted to be with people in their suffering, at birth, and at death. According to Dom Helder, "I was born to be a priest . . . I have a chapel inside me. I guess I'm a long way from being a mystic, but still there are moments when I go aside like a monk."[3] However, his greatest attribute for the priesthood has been his love of life. Dom Helder has confessed, ". . . I like the sun and water and people and life. Life is beautiful, and I often wonder why to preserve life we have to kill other lives . . . ."[4] There has always been a poetic side to this priest's life. He revels in the metaphor, and he finds his imagination to be a great teacher. Dom Helder has said of imagination:

> You know imagination is very important in understanding creation, it helps us to understand God. Once when the ants had eaten the leaves of my rose-bush I picked up an ant and scolded it for doing so. But the ant in my palm taught me a lesson. As it squirmed in my hand it replied: "Why should you be the only one to enjoy the rose-bush?"[5]

This sense of fascination with all of God's creation has followed Dom Helder throughout his life.

During the 1920s Dom Helder received his education at the Seminary of Sao Jose in Fortaleza. In those years the main interests of the Brazilian church concerned religious indifference, religious ignorance, the lack of integration between religion and life, and the threat of communism. Dom Helder was taught that the church's major function in society was to preserve the social order. The only social issue he heard addressed in seminary was the political confrontation of capitalism and communism. In Dom Helder's words: "When I left the seminary. . . . I had the impression that the world was increasingly divided into two opposing camps: Capitalism and Communism."[6] The issue of poverty and the rights of peasants in Brazilian life were not on the church's agenda.

The church was clearly preoccupied with the matter of preserving Brazilian society against the perceived threat of the godless Communists. In the early 1930s, a Brazilian form of fascism came into existence with the avowed purpose of celebrating "God, the fatherland, and the family" as an antidote to communism. These Integralists, as the Fascists called themselves, modeled their political philosophy after the work of European fascists such as Hitler, Mussolini, and Salazar. Many young Brazilian intellectuals were attracted to Integralism because it promised to revitalize the national spirit of Brazil. It was to this group that Dom Helder Camara gravitated as a new priest fresh out of seminary. He liked Integralism's emphasis upon wedding the values of church and family with the state. However, Dom Helder's fascination with Brazilian fascism was short-lived after he discovered the darker side of the movement. Those who were not with the Integralists were accused of being unpatriotic and un-Christian. Dom Helder became increasingly uncomfortable with the mean spirit of the Fascists.

In 1934 Dom Helder was called to Rio de Janeiro to work on the espiscopal staff of Cardinal Lemme, one of Brazil's most famous religious leaders. He was asked by Lemme to abandon his connections with the Integralists which he did quite happily. During the next several decades Dom Helder established his reputation as an educator and an effective bureaucrat. He probably would have lived out a distinguished but unspectacular religious career had it not been for an event that came to be pivotal to Dom Helder in 1955.

In that year the city of Rio was to be the site for the Roman Catholic Church's International Eucharistic Congress. This congress was held every four years in different parts of the world. It would attract thousands upon thousands of Catholics from every nation on the globe. The cardinal who resided in Rio at this time, Jaime Camara (no relation), asked Dom Helder to organize the entire event. The congress was a tremendous success, and most of the credit for the success was given to Dom Helder Camara. In addition to the congress, Dom Helder had also made the arrangements for the first meeting of the Latin American bishops who met immediately after the congress ended. He was elected secretary general of this group which would later become CELAM (The powerful Bishop's Council for the whole of South America).

Dom Helder Camara became something of a celebrity in Rio de Janeiro, for he had brought international recognition to his city. It was in this context that the highly respected Cardinal Gerlier of France sought out Dom Helder at the close of the congress. Gerlier had taken the tour of Rio's slums (the *favelas*), which had been arranged by the church to draw attention to some of the human problems in Brazil's major city. Expecting more praise for the success of the congress, Dom Helder was surprised and humbled by Cardinal Gerlier's remarks. Here is a portion of Dom Helder's own account of this historic meeting.

. . . He (Gerlier) shut the door before telling me the purpose of his visit.

"I have had some experience in organization," he said, "and since taking part in this Eucharistic Congress I must tell you that you have exceptional capacities as an organizer. This is not a compliment I am paying you. I say it instead to awaken you to a sense of responsibility. Now, I ask you: Why do you not put those capacities of yours to work at solving the problems of the slums, what you call the *favelas*?[7]

Dom Helder then reported that he turned to Cardinal Gerlier and kissed his hands. "This," he said, "is a turning point in my life! I will dedicate myself to the poor!"[8]

Cardinal Gerlier had ignited Dom Helder's desire to work with the poor, he had given new birth to his moral conscience. It took this word from another, spoken in loving confrontation, to awaken Dom Helder's love for the dispossessed. And once awakened, he was not to be denied his mission with the poor. Through the Crusade of St. Sebastian, led by Dom Helder, ten large apartment blocks in Rio were built to replace the slum dwellings. Within less than a year thousands of people from the *favelas* had been relocated in new apartment centers which included schools, kindergartens, and social halls.[9] However, as Dom Helder soon discovered, the newly vacated slums were quickly reinhabited by more poor people from the countryside, peasants who had come to the city looking for work. The population of the *favelas* could not be reduced, and it was not long before this energetic priest realized that the problems of Rio's slums were directly linked to Brazil's overall failure to create just laws for the fair treatment of the nation's peasant population. The economic and social exploitation of the poor by Brazil's wealthy establishment simply perpetuated the existence of slums.

There was no clean water, no sanitation, and few roads within the *favelas*, but Dom Helder realized that a response to these basic human needs meant nothing without social justice. The slum dwellers had no rights. They had no voice in government. They were not permitted to organize for their own benefit; often they were not even aware that they were entitled to basic human rights. They had accepted their society's definition of them as nonpersons. It was in this atmosphere that Dom Helder established grass-roots communities among the poor so that they might begin to exercise some degree of personal autonomy. Fatalism seemed to be the worst enemy of the slums. The people had no belief or expectation that they could effect change for the improvement of the quality of their own lives. Gradually Dom Helder and his co-workers helped the people of the *favelas* gain self-confidence. They were helping the people of the slums to empower themselves. However, when the voice of discontent began to be heard from the slums, the wealthy landowners and their government bureaucrats became very nervous. The original goodwill which had been extended to Dom Helder for his slum work was withdrawn. He had stepped over the line. He was no longer asking for charity; he was seeking justice.

The Social Witness

For those who become social witnesses for justice, there comes a point at which the prophetic stance causes alienation. Even close friends become uncomfortable with the prophet's uncompromising stance on issues of justice. In Dom Helder's case, his personal friendship with his superior, Cardinal Camara became strained. The cardinal loved and respected Dom Helder, but his conservative politics and his fear of communism made him more and more wary of Dom Helder's social activism.

A break in their friendship came during a solemn mass celebrated in honor of St. Vincent de Paul. When Dom Helder was asked by Cardinal Camara to pronounce the eulogy for St. Vincent, he seized this moment to make a public witness for the cause of the poor. According to Dom Helder's account:

> I tried to say that the important thing to remember about Saint Vincent is not what he did—for this is well known and needs none of our praise. Instead, we should meditate on the question: What would Saint Vincent de Paul do today? What would be the principal manifestations of his charity? To sum up: Saint Vincent de Paul's charity today would be to do justice.[10]

This public challenge to the church to do justice could not be tolerated. Cardinal Camara decided that it was time for he and Dom Helder to part company. As Dom Helder recalls: "The time had come for us to part. Dom Jaime, who had always treated me honourably, spoke to me like a father, honestly and explicitly. 'My son, we must part as Paul and Barnabas did and remain brothers.'"[11]

In 1964 Dom Helder Camara was promoted upstairs to keep him out of trouble. He was made an archbishop, but he was sent back to his home province in the northeast. This served only to increase the scope and dimension of Dom Helder's social witness, for he was placed in the heart of Brazilian poverty. Here he was resolved to identify the church fully with the cause of social justice. Even as an archbishop he would side with the poor. His situation was seriously complicated by a military coup which toppled Brazil's fragile democracy. It was clear that the new junta would not tolerate the public presence of social reformers. They were labeled "Communists."

Dom Helder knew that he must speak out against the potential repression of this new regime. The cry for justice among the poor could not be silenced. He understood that he must speak: "I seized the occasion [his installation ceremony] to speak out my thoughts very clearly, knowing that if God did not give me the courage at that time, at my entrance into the diocese, afterward it would be too late."[12] In his speech the new archbishop identified himself with the poor. He told his people, "It is clear that, loving everyone, I must have a special love, like Christ,

for the poor."[13] He committed himself, and his church, to work
for social justice. He asserted:

> Continuing the existing work of our archdiocese, I shall care for
> the poor, being particularly concerned that poverty should not
> degenerate into misery. Poverty can and at times must be accepted
> generously or offered spontaneously as a gift to the Father. But
> misery is degrading and repellent; it destroys the image of God
> which is in each of us; it violates the right and duty of human
> beings to strive for personal fulfillment.[14]

Dom Helder alerted his fellow citizens: "If we wish to tackle
the roots of our social evils, we must help our country to break
the vicious circle of underdevelopment and misery."[15] The new
military regime considered these statements of the new archbishop to be inflammatory and seditious. They became even
more concerned when Dom Helder pledged to have dialogue
with all manner of people—those on the political left and the
political right, the revolutionaries and the reactionaries. The day
following these public pronouncements by Dom Helder his episcopal headquarters was invaded by members of the Fourth Army
as a show of force.

Dom Helder was not to be deterred. He was committed to an
identification with the poor. He ordered the ornate episcopal
palace in Recife to be transformed into a hall for the people. The
huge episcopal thrones were removed, and the doors and win-
dows of this stuffy old building were literally thrown open for
all to enter. Dom Helder himself chose to live outside the episcopal palace. As soon as he received ecclesiastical permission,
he had the sacristy of a local church partitioned into a small
three-room apartment for his dwelling place. He would have
no housekeeper, and he would answer his own door and tele-
phone. There were to be no servants.

In his own personal demeanor Dom Helder chose to convey
simplicity as a mark of his solidarity with the poor. He preferred
to dress in the traditional cassock of the priesthood without the
purple trimmings which accompanied the office of the archbishop. The only religious symbol he wore was a plain wooden
cross which hung from his neck by a metal chain.[16] The journalist
Oriana Fallaci has said of Dom Helder:

The little old man is pale and balding, with the look of a country parish priest.
But this is no country priest, no little old man. He is one of the most important men you could meet in Brazil or in all Latin America, and perhaps the most intelligent and plucky too.[17]

Like other priests, Dom Helder had taken vows of poverty, chastity, and obedience. However, his commitment to the poor added yet another vow—the vow of simplicity. Dom Helder had exercised a candor and honesty which is completely disarming. The truth is to be spoken in an unencumbered way.

When Dom Helder was accused by a Brazilian general of selling out to the Communists, he met the accusation head on. He went directly to his accuser and asked him why he was persecuting him with such lies. In Dom Helder's words:

I once put the question directly to a general: "Why do you call me a Communist? Why do you persecute not just Dom Helder but everyone who is working and fighting for human advancement, calling them Communists and subversives?" And he replied: "It's very simple. It's much easier and quicker to open people's eyes than to carry out reforms, do you know that? If you do know it, and you continue to open people's eyes and spread ideas. . . . you are obviously an agitator and a subversive.[18]

According to the general's definition, anyone who helped raise the consciousness of the poor was to be regarded as a Communist and a subversive. Dom Helder was aware that by this definition he was guilty as charged, but he would not let the general's statement go by unchallenged. In a prophetic inversion of values, Dom Helder made his counterpoint: "You call me an agitator, a subversive? The very situation in which the people live is subversive!"[19]

Dom Helder's life has been endangered many times because of his prophetic stance. For many, he is a man who must not live. A reactionary political group called the CCC (Comando Caca-Comunistas) has made several attempts on his life. This clandestine terrorist group was opposed to anyone in Brazil who advocated social change, and it functioned as a murder squad for the military junta.

Dom Helder has reported the attempts which have been made upon his life by the CCC to the international press.

This CCC has honored me several times; twice here in my house, where they ruined the walls with machine-gun bullets and filthied the church wall; once in my episcopal palace, once in a Catholic institute, and another time in a church where I frequently officiate. Besides, they shot a student I know in the spine with machine-gun bullets and now he is paralyzed for life. One of my assistants, a 27-year-old priest, was hung from a tree and riddled with gun shots. These things, in Recife, hardly cause surprise anymore.[20]

By 1970 the Brazilian government itself had decided to silence Dom Helder, but not by murder. Its method was much more subtle; government officials knew of the archbishop's popularity among the people, and they did not want to create a revolutionary martyr, so they decided to erase his name from the public record. In a systematic way Dom Helder was slandered in the national press. He was labeled a traitor and a Communist sympathizer. Then a ban of silence was imposed. Dom Helder's name was not permitted to be mentioned on radio, television, or in the press. In addition, he was not permitted to defend himself against the various charges of sedition. He had become a nonperson in the eyes of the state. The name of Dom Helder Camara simply disappeared from national life. In 1975 the silenced archbishop told a foreign correspondent: "I was and am condemned to civil death. I do not exist."[21]

A New Consciousness

Although he was effectively silenced in his own country, Dom Helder knew that the truth could not ultimately be suppressed. He lived with the confidence that the cry for social justice would continue to be heard, and indeed he was correct. At the very time his witness was censored in Brazil, it began to gain international recognition. During the 1970s Dom Helder's prophetic words concerning poverty and economic repression made their way around the world. On the basis of his courageous witness for justice in Brazil, he was nominated for the Nobel Peace Prize. In 1970 he received the Martin Luther King, Jr., Award for keeping alive the quest for social justice and world peace. By the time of his retirement as archbishop of Olinda and Recife in 1984, Dom Helder's voice was once again being heard within Brazil due to the most recent democratization of Brazilian politics.

Dom Helder's works were translated into Spanish and English. In the Third World his name was identified with liberation and revolution. His rejection of the imperialism of both the United States and the Soviet Union made him a popular speaker in Third World countries. His grasp of the dynamics of Latin American politics and the need for social justice was matched only by a deep spiritual commitment to transform his world of poverty into a world of dignity and hope.

At the very center of Dom Helder's message we can discover a call for change. This change is meant to be a radical change in which our very perception of reality is transformed. Dom Helder calls us to the development of a new consciousness. The old consciousness, which most of us maintain, is destructive because it supports the status quo which in turn preserves many of the injustices that need to be overcome. Since Dom Helder is first and foremost a priest, this desire to establish a new consciousness has a theological basis.

In relation to theological doctrine, for example, Dom Helder believes that it is necessary to rethink all the major themes of the Christian faith in relation to a global need for social justice and lasting peace. Beginning with the doctrine of creation, we should recapture the important mandate to be co-creators with God. In the Genesis stories, we are given tremendous responsibilities. We are to name the living creatures, we are to take care of the earth, and to preserve the dignity of our own species. Unfortunately some have understood our creative calling to be a license for exploitation—exploitation of natural resources and exploitation of other human beings. But Dom Helder claims that that was not God's intent. Our charge is to be co-creators; we are not to destroy but to create, to give life, not to take life.

Likewise, according to the Gospel of the New Testament, we are to stand for life. The work of redemption concerns the affirmation of life and a denial of the forces of death. As with creation, redemption is a life process initiated by God, but it is a life process in which we also participate. We are called to love as God loved us in Jesus—this is the work of redemption, and we are to minister to all of God's creation seeking to insure that God's joyful intent for our well-being is accomplished among all people. This means to liberate the oppressed. It means to free the oppressor. It means to lift the life of all those who now know only a living death. It means to work for the restoration of the physical, emotional, and spiritual health of every human being.[22]

According to Dom Helder, we should be transformed by our theology. We should be led to a new consciousness. The incarnation of Christ revealed the change which God has dared to suggest for each of our own lives. In the incarnation, God chose to be "in-fleshed" in Jesus of Nazareth. God teaches us through the incarnation that we too must become incarnate. God got involved and so we, too, should get involved. God's love and healing must be incarnate, that is, it must find its expression in specific situations and in concrete circumstances. In Dom Helder's words, we need to "become incarnate in our own particular Nazareth."[23]

We in North America, for example, must be sensitized to how our government and economy affect the poor of Dom Helder's world. It is important that we understand the kind of influence our country's policies of aid and development have had on places like Latin America. Dom Helder has asked us to consider the consequences of a decade of development in the 1960s when the United States invested over three billion dollars in Latin America, while it made a profit of eleven billion dollars from those same neighbors.[24] From our perspective we might consider that kind of transaction a good business venture which returned a healthy profit. However, viewed from the vantage point of the poor of Latin America, it is the worst form of exploitation. The so-called development dollars helped the already rich, the landed aristocracy, and the corrupt government officials. The poor continued to be poor and as a matter of fact they became poorer. Dom Helder has written:

> Sadly, the noble idea of development became degraded, robbed of its original meaning. Very soon in Brazil, as with everywhere else, development came to mean simply economic growth: people didn't see that it brought profit only to the privileged classes, and that it was achieved at the cost of further proletarization of the masses. That's why we now prefer, in Brazil and the rest of Latin America, to speak of 'liberation'. . . .[25]

The question for those of us in North America who profess an incarnational (Christ-centered) faith is whether or not we are capable of embracing a new perspective which will permit us to view reality from the perspective of the poor. As long as we in the developed nations do not see the connections between economic growth and social justice, the situation in Latin America will not improve. We must begin to understand ourselves as part of the problem!

Dom Helder is committed to the continuation of his work of consciousness raising (demystification) within the context of his own country, but he is convinced that we in North America must also change. We need to be better educated to the problems of Latin America as viewed from a perspective other than our own economic and national interests. Dom Helder continues to believe very deeply that hearts and minds can be changed—even ours. He has confessed: "I may be a utopian and naive, but I say it is possible to conscientize the masses and perhaps even start a dialogue with the oppressors. No one is completely wicked."[26] This may indeed sound like a naive assumption, but Dom Helder has been willing to risk his life on this belief. Can we do the same in our "Nazareth"?

The Spiral of Violence

For Dom Helder the greatest obstacle to social and economic change is the excessive violence of our age. We might develop a new consciousness, but unless we deal with the violence which permeates our societies, we will not be able to advance to justice. In his public witness Dom Helder has had to confront directly the issue of violence—the violence of the political system, the violence of terrorists on both the left and the right, the violence of racism and classism. The violence of his own heart.

In response, the archbishop of Recife has chosen the path of nonviolence. Without question he counts himself among the revolutionaries of Latin America, but unlike many of his contemporaries he continues to advocate nonviolence as both a moral conviction and a political strategy. At the very basis of this commitment to nonviolence is his dedication to the teachings of Jesus. He has read both Mahatma Gandhi and Martin Luther King, but his nonviolent approach traces its roots to the gospel of Christ itself. He has said of his commitment to non-violence:

> This personal position is founded on the Gospel. . . . We need
> only turn to the Beatitudes—the quintessence of the Gospel mes-
> sage—to see that the option for Christians is clear. We, as Chris-
> tians, are on the side of nonviolence, and this is in no way an
> option for weakness and passivity. Opting for nonviolence means
> to believe more strongly in the power of truth, justice, and love
> than in the power of wars, weapons, and hatred.[27]

Dom Helder knows that the use of nonviolence as a tactic for
social change can be very costly. He understands that the moral
agent of nonviolence must be willing to take the violence of
others upon himself or herself. He has cautioned his friends
that the way of nonviolence for the sake of justice and peace is
a lonely path: "We must not expect to find it easy; we shall not
walk on roses, people will not throng to hear us and applaud,
and we shall not always be aware of divine protection. If we
are to be pilgrims for justice and peace, we must expect the
desert."[28]

There is no other way but the way of the "desert." A witness
must be made against the vicious spiral of violence. According
to Dom Helder, the roots of social violence can be found in the
inequitable distribution of wealth. He calls this form of structural
violence "Violence No. 1." The poor experience this insidious
brand of violence daily. It has many names; it can be called
hunger, or ignorance, or exploitation, or misery, or hopeless-
ness. By definition the subhuman living conditions of the poor
are violent. This kind of violence is pervasive in the life of the
"have nots." It constantly saps life from the poor. Unfair laws
and government policies often contribute to this Violence No.
1. It is also exacerbated by plain old-fashioned greed. In many
ways this is a hidden form of violence. It is the violence of which
we do not speak.

A second form of violence, referred to as Violence No. 2 by
Dom Helder, is much more visible to the public eye. This form
of violence is a reaction to Violence No. 1 and it contributes to
violence's spiral effect. Out of sheer frustration and often out
of blind rage the victims of Violence No. 1 rebel against the
dehumanizing conditions under which they live. They rise up

in anger. This violent reaction of the victims is frequently spontaneous, indiscriminate, and harmful to the victims themselves. Ironically, this stage in the spiral of violence is sometimes identified in the popular press as the time when "things turned violent." In truth, however, Violence No. 2 is a direct result of the preexisting violence of economic, social, and political repression.

The spiral of violence continues. The violent rebellion of the dispossessed and the oppressed must now be put down by new means of violence. This Violence No. 3 is organized violence. It is the violence of the state exercised to restore "law and order." Very often this form of violence is given to excesses, and the most devastating aspect of Violence No. 3 is that it is visited upon the victims of Violence No. 1. The poor lose in a very big way! In Dom Helder's estimate:

> When conflict comes out into the streets, when violence No. 2 tries to resist violence No. 1, the authorities consider themselves obliged to preserve or re-establish public order, even if this means using force; this is violence No. 3. Sometimes they go even further, and this is becoming increasingly common: in order to obtain information . . . the logic of violence leads them to use moral and physical torture. . . .[29]

The pattern has been set; there is simply no end to the spiral of violence. The only way to stop the spiral is to confront the issues which cause Violence No. 1. Only when justice is served will violence cease.

The Abrahamic Minorities

As a witness for social change, Dom Helder has an alternative for violence. He envisions the development of communities of justice and peace around the world. These communities are made up of men and women of good will from various religious and philosophical backgrounds. They are people who are willing to work in a nonviolent manner for peace and justice within their societies. Dom Helder claims that those groups already exist, at least in part. He calls them the "Abrahamic minorities." Like Abraham of the Old Testament, these communities are prepared to take risks. They are willing to strike out on their own journeys. Like Abraham, these people hope against hope that what they do will make a difference.

The future, Dom Helder believes, belongs in the hands of the Abrahamic minorities. Drawing from his own experiences, he can find little hope in institutions or in governments. He has written: "At one time I believed that institutions could be converted. . . . But that was an impossible dream. Today I realize that the ways of the Lord are not exactly our ways. My hope lies now in grassroots communities."[30] It is the committed private citizens of the world who will make the difference. The work of doing justice belongs to the peoples of the world, not their governments.

During the 1970s, Dom Helder set about creating Abrahamic minorities in Brazil. He established a network of people called "Action for Justice and Peace." In this movement Dom Helder sought to enlist 15 percent of Brazil's bishops who, in their turn, would recruit 15 percent of Brazil's priests, who, in their turn, would mobilize 15 percent of Brazil's Roman Catholic laity. Dom Helder succeeded! Many non-Catholics were also added to the ranks of this nonviolent movement. These people and their early experimental prototypes engaged in public demonstrations for social justice in Brazil as early as 1968.[31]

The philosophy of Dom Helder's Abrahamic minority movement was based, as we might imagine, upon the lives of Jesus, Gandhi, and King. In one of the foundational documents of "Action for Justice and Peace," Dom Helder reproduced the pledge created by Martin Luther King, Jr., for his American civil rights movement. Those of us who seek to do justice in our society might do well to consider this pledge.

I hereby pledge myself—my person and my body—to the nonviolent movement. Therefore, I will keep the following Ten Commandments:

1. Meditate daily on the teachings and life of Jesus.

2. Remember always that the nonviolent movement . . . seeks justice and reconciliation, not victory.

3. Walk and talk in the manner of love, for God is love.

4. Pray daily to be used by God in order that all men might be free.

5. Sacrifice personal wishes in order that all men might be free.

6. Observe with both friend and foe the ordinary rules of courtesy.

7. Seek to perform regular service for others and for the world.

8. Refrain from the violence of fist, tongue, or heart.

9. Strive to be in good spiritual and bodily health.

10. Follow the directions of the movement and of the captain on a demonstration.[32]

Dom Helder is convinced that the Abrahamic minorities of the world cannot be silenced. He also realizes that the mission of the Abrahamic minorities will take a special kind of person. He has said:

It is only those who achieve an inner unity within themselves and possess a worldwide vision and universal spirit who will be fit instruments to perform the miracle of combining the violence of the prophets, the truth of Christ, the revolutionary spirit of the gospel—but without destroying love.[33]

As for himself, Dom Helder will continue his witness for social justice. He knows that his life is in constant danger, but he says he will not hide. In his typical straightforward fashion, he leaves us with these personal thoughts: "If God wants me killed, I accept that as a grace: maybe my death could be helpful. I've lost almost all my hair, the few I still have are white, and I have only a few more years to live. Threats don't scare me. It is hard to shut me up by threatening. The only judge I accept is God."[34]

How Can We Do Justice?

Through the life and thought of Dom Helder Camara, we have been introduced to a modern-day prophet. He has exposed us to the need for social justice among the poor of Brazil and by extension to the needs of all those who suffer from oppression around the globe. We have been taught several important lessons. In the first place, if we are to do justice, we must be willing to become personal witnesses for justice. As witnesses we will need to prepare ourselves for the alienation that results from our taking a stand. Like Dom Helder, our character will be maligned; we will be harassed; and we may even be killed. In this sense our idealism must be tempered by a realism which recognizes the personal costs of witnessing for justice.

In the second place, it is important to note that doing justice requires the development of a new consciousness. As with Dom Helder, we will have to rethink our faith and our values. We will need to look at life from the perspective of the world's poor. And if we are genuinely serious about our commitment to social justice, we will have to accept the fact that the victim's point of view has more relevance and reality than our own. With Dom Helder we will need to seek to identify with the poor, the dispossessed, and the outcast. Our life-style will need to be changed so that we can share in the simplicity and dignity of God's blessed people—the poor of the earth.

Third, if we are to do justice, we must deal with the terrible spiral of violence which threatens to destroy us all. We need to continue to witness against the threat of a nuclear holocaust, but we also need to be aware of what Dom Helder calls the "poverty bomb." The continued existence of poverty and hunger among the majority of the world's population is violence on a grand scale. The East-West confrontation, in the long run, may not be as frightening as the North-South confrontation over dwindling resources. We must avoid a cataclysmic war between the wealthy "few" and the majority of our planet's population which will have less and less.

Finally, in doing justice it is essential that we join hands with others who have given themselves to the cause of social justice and its wonderful fruit—lasting peace. Following Dom Helder, we would do well to identify ourselves with joyful Abrahamic minorities—with people of faith and vision who hold justice and peace to be a highest priority. In the final analysis the archbishop of Recife and Olinda presents us with a tremendous challenge of the will—a challenge to which he really believes we can respond. The question is really not how do we do justice, but rather do we have the will to want to do justice? Dom Helder Camara says yes! His entire life is a statement to that effect.

Recommended Readings

Dom Helder Camara
  Spiral of Violence. London: Sheed and Ward, 1971.

The Desert is Fertile. Maryknoll, N.Y.: Orbis Books, 1974.
The Conversions of a Bishop: An Interview with José de Broucker. London: Collins, 1979.

Books about Dom Helder Camara

José de Broucker, *Dom Helder Camara: The Violence of a Peacemaker.* Maryknoll, N.Y.: Orbis Books, 1970.

Bernhard Moosbrugger and Gladys Weigner, *Voice of the Third World: Dom Helder Camara.* New York: Pyramid Publications, 1972.

NOTES

[1] Mary Hall, *The Impossible Dream: The Spirituality of Dom Helder Camara* (Maryknoll, N.Y.: Orbis Books, 1980), p. 62.
[2] *Ibid.*, p. 23.
[3] Dom Helder Camara, *Helder Camara: Talks and Writings* (Washington, D.C.: Latin American Documentation, 1975), p. 7.
[4] *Ibid.*
[5] Mary Hall, *The Impossible Dream*, p. 67.
[6] Dom Helder Camara, *The Conversions of a Bishop: An Interview with José de Broucker* (London: Collins, 1979), p. 46.
[7] *Ibid.* p. 152.
[8] *Ibid.*
[9] Bernhard Moosbrugger and Gladys Weigner, *Voice of the Third World: Dom Helder Camara* (New York: Pyramid Publications, 1972), p. 23.
[10] José de Broucker, *Dom Helder Camara: The Violence of a Peacemaker* (Maryknoll, N.Y.: Orbis Books, 1970), pp. 152-153.
[11] Mary Hall, *The Impossible Dream*, pp. 71-72.
[12] José de Broucker, *Dom Helder Camara: The Violence of a Peacemaker*, p. 154.
[13] Dom Helder Camara, *The Church and Colonialism: The Betrayal of the Third World* (Denville, N.J.: Dimension Books, 1969), p. 6.
[14] *Ibid.*
[15] *Ibid.*, p. 7.
[16] Mary Hall, *The Impossible Dream*, p. 16.
[17] Dom Helder Camara, *Helder Camara: Talks and Writings*, p. 1.
[18] Dom Helder Camara, *The Conversions of a Bishop*, p. 90.
[19] *Ibid.*
[20] Dom Helder Camara, *Helder Camara: Talks and Writings*, p. 3.
[21] Dom Helder Camara, *The Conversions of a Bishop*, p. 200.
[22] Dom Helder's theology of life in contrast to the forces of death is captured by Mary Hall in her biography of Camara entitled *The Impossible Dream: The Spirituality of Dom Helder Camara.*
[23] *Ibid.*, p. 121.
[24] Bernhard Moosbrugger and Gladys Weigner, *Voice of the Third World: Dom Helder Camara*, p. 16.
[25] Dom Helder Camara, *The Conversions of a Bishop*, p. 89.
[26] Dom Helder Camara, *Helder Camara: Talks and Writings*, p. 6.

[27] José de Broucker, *Dom Helder Camara: The Violence of a Peacemaker*, p. 57.

[28] Dom Helder Camara, *The Desert is Fertile* (Maryknoll, N.Y.: Orbis Books, 1974), p. 24.

[29] Dom Helder Camara, *Spiral of Violence* (London: Sheed and Ward, 1971), p. 34.

[30] Dom Helder Camara, *The Conversions of a Bishop*, p. 120.

[31] José de Broucker, *Dom Helder Camara: The Violence of a Peacemaker*, pp. 58-65.

[32] *Ibid.* pp. 57-58.

[33] Dom Helder Camara, *The Church and Colonialism*, p. 111.

[34] Dom Helder Camara, *Helder Camara: Talks and Writings*, p. 8.

7

MARK HATFIELD:
What Is Peace?

Their feet run to evil, and they make haste to shed
    innocent blood;
their thoughts are thoughts of iniquity, desolation
    and destruction are in their highways.
The way of peace they know not, and there is no justice
    in their paths;
They have made their roads crooked, no one who goes
    in them knows peace.
                           —Isaiah 59:7-8

Blessed are the peacemakers, for they shall be called
    sons of God.
                           —Matthew 5:9

What is peace? This is a question which our generation asks so often, but of which it knows so little. The Bible, in both its testaments, has much to say about the issue of peace. Granted, its pages are also filled with accounts of wars and violence—battles being waged between nations, and between powers and principalities not exclusively of this world. However, in their highest moral and spiritual expressions, the Scriptures tell us about a peaceful kingdom. The Old Testament prophets and Jesus have pictured an emerging kingdom of God's peace (shalom). In fact the early followers of Jesus believed that their Lord himself embodied God's shalom in his earthly ministry and in his resurrected life.

The biblical concept of the peaceful kingdom certainly provides us with a grand vision of a way of life much unlike our present existence. We are introduced to a creative way of living in which there is a commitment to the well-being of all God's creation. According to the Sermon on the Mount, true happiness (blessedness) comes to those who embrace the way of shalom. Blessed are the peacemakers! Indeed, those called to follow Jesus are called to be co-creators of peace with God. Making peace, establishing shalom, is at the very heart of the Christian life.

Today, many people desire to "keep" the peace. Few people want war. Therefore, great efforts are made to guard the peace, which primarily means to prevent the outbreak of war. But who actually works toward peace? Who is willing to pursue peace as a constructive vision? Who is willing to envision peace as more than simply the absence of armed conflict? The Christian, following the biblical concept of God's shalom, should be well suited for this task. Those who claim the name of Christ are encouraged by their Lord to invest their lives in "the things which make for peace" (Luke 19:42).

Mark O. Hatfield, United States Senator from Oregon, is an example of one who has committed his life to peacemaking in the name of Christ. He has dared to take his advocacy for peace into the halls of Congress. In his words and actions he has attempted to disclose to others the radical dimensions of God's shalom which know no boundaries in the pursuit of peace. In a recent interview with the senator I asked him what he understood his life to be all about. "If you could put your life's concern in the form of a question," I asked, "what would that question be?" After a lengthy, thoughtful pause, he answered, "My question is this, what is peace?"[1] This is the question which has been at the center of Hatfield's entire career as a public servant, and it is the question that has penetrated the core of his Christian existence.

Always respected, often alone, the senior senator from Oregon has consistently challenged the American people to accept the role of peacemaker in today's world. Those who seek to follow Christ and those interested in peacemaking could find no better guide than Mark Hatfield. His Christian witness in this area is unparalleled among our current national leaders. As a Christian layperson and as an elected official of our government, he speaks clearly and boldly about "the things which make for peace."

Hiroshima

On August 7, 1945, the Japanese city of Hiroshima was destroyed by an American atomic bomb. For Mark Hatfield this date has more than a passing historical interest. It is the time in which everything changed. After Hiroshima, the world would never be the same again—nor would Hatfield. In September, 1945, along with other U.S. Navy observers, he entered the devastated city of Hiroshima. He has never forgotten what he saw that day.

The results of the bomb's destruction were beyond Hatfield's comprehension. He has written of this experience in *Conflict and Conscience*:

> The devastation I saw at Hiroshima seemed beyond the comprehension of my mind and spirit; I felt jarred in the depth of my soul. I was witnessing the effects of a horror too terrible to imagine. Never would I be the same again; the shock to my conscience registered permanently within me.[2]

Many of the estimated 78,150 victims of the bomb had not yet been buried. The "survivors" had uncertain futures; many of them would die from the effects of radiation exposure. Thousands of other citizens of Hiroshima were simply listed as missing. Hatfield recalls looking on in horror as some of the men in his detail pulled teeth with gold fillings from the mouths of dead Japanese for souvenirs and pierced earrings.[3] The bomb had erased all respect for human life.

A lesson must be learned from Hiroshima. We are in a new age—one in which the bomb *has* been used and could be used again. Hatfield has dedicated his life to the prevention of the future use of such weapons. But the struggle is clearly an uphill battle. According to Senator Hatfield, our government alone has the technological capabilities to release the equivalent explosive power of 655,000 Hiroshima bombs. He has noted: "The United States can, in a matter of moments, deliver a single, thermonuclear explosion with more destructive power than both sides dropped against each other during the four and a half years of World War II."[4]

In our nuclear age the task of peacemaking has an urgency about it that the world has never known before. We are literally on the brink of destruction. We need to listen to the voices of those working for peace. And we must look deeply inside ourselves to understand how it is that we block the entrance of peace into our own lives. Peacemaking, although it is a global task, has to begin somewhere, and it best begin with ourselves. This is the truth which Mark Hatfield discovered at Hiroshima on his way to becoming a peacemaker.

Portrait of a Peacemaker

As important as the experience of Hiroshima was for Hatfield's development as a peacemaker, the pivotal point in his conversion to peacemaking came at another time and, in another place. We are speaking of Hatfield's conversion to Jesus Christ. Raised in a Christian home and exposed to the Bible at an early age, the senator nevertheless did not come into a personal relationship with Christ until his thirty-first year. This proved to be the turning point of his life. But before we discuss this event, it is helpful to survey other significant events which led up to the conversion experience. Hatfield has recognized what many others have discovered about their relationship with God. Before we can find God, God has already found us. He has written in this regard:

> When one looks back upon his own spiritual pilgrimage, he often senses that it has not only been his personal search for God, but also God's search for him—seeking, pursuing, and finally grasping him. Although one's encounter with the Person of Christ is a process of continual growth and change, there are often pivotal points which become markers along the path.[5]

An important marker along Hatfield's spiritual journey was his family. Hatfield's father was a quiet, reserved man who took great pride in his vocation as a blacksmith. In the senator's estimate his father was a deeply spiritual individual who was very much at peace with himself and his world. He was content to accept life as it came to him, and he was very sensitive to the presence of God. Hatfield's mother, on the other hand, was an activist. She was a "doer" with a tremendous amount of ambition. She was not the contemplative that her husband was.[6]

While Hatfield was a young boy, during the time of the Great Depression, his mother decided to get a teaching degree. With the support of the small Hatfield family—Mark was an only child—she set off for Oregon State University to enroll in education courses. For the next several years she lived on the Corvallis campus while her husband and son remained behind at the Dallas, Oregon, homestead. With the assistance of Hatfield's maternal grandmother, the Hatfields managed to survive until the teaching degree was earned and the family was once again fully united.

Hatfield's mother had high ambitions for her son. She wanted him to have an education, to experience the world, and to make a name for himself. In Hatfield's words, "She wanted me to be something more than a blacksmith, and she pushed me along."[7] Such ambitions were not intended as a criticism of her husband's profession, for Hatfield's mother had tremendous respect for his father's craft. The point was that she wanted something "different" for her son. It was clear that young Mark was not cut out for the work of blacksmithing. As a child he was not physically strong, and his interests were mostly intellectual; reading and studying history were his favorite pastimes.

Hatfield looked forward to his involvement in mealtime discussions around the family table. And in the Hatfield household this invariably meant a discussion of politics. The Hatfields had tremendous admiration for the great statesmen of American politics; in fact, young Mark's heroes included nearly as many political figures as cowboys and athletes.[8] By the time he had reached high school, he was well on his way to a political career. According to Hatfield himself: "From the time I was a high school student I participated in political campaigns as either a full-time volunteer or a paid employee."[9]

In the years which followed, Hatfield's early interest in politics led to a political career. After graduating from Willamette University, he served in the Navy during World War II, then he returned to school receiving an advanced degree in political science from Stanford. He was subsequently invited back to Willamette to teach political science and later served as dean of

students. But his eyes were on the political arena. While still on
the Willamette faculty, he ran for a seat in the Oregon House
of Representatives and won!

In 1950, at the age of twenty-eight, Mark Hatfield became the
youngest member of the Oregon House. He was also the first
academic professor to be elected to the Oregon legislature since
1917. For several years he held positions both at Willamette and
in the legislature. Then, in 1955, he decided to run for the office
of secretary of state of Oregon. His victory in this election paved
the path to the governorship which he held for two terms beginning in 1958 and ending in 1966 when he was elected to the
United States Senate.

It was clear to Hatfield that politics had always been the
natural outlet for his commitment to something beyond himself.
In *Conflict and Conscience* he has indicated that political involvement was the logical consequence of what he taught in the
classroom.

> In politics, for example, it was easy for me to see the value of
> commitment. In fact, I used to expound it to my classes when I
> was a political science teacher at Willamette University in Salem,
> Oregon.
> "Take a stand!" . . . "Join a party, meet the candidates, ring
> door bells, get involved." . . . "Get down off the bleachers and
> into the rough-and-tumble where the issues of life are decided."[10]

However, while still at Willamette and in the Oregon House,
Hatfield had begun to wonder about another kind of commitment—his commitment to his faith in Jesus Christ.

As a dean of students, and as a legislator, he found himself
dealing with the personal problems of others. He grew increasingly uncomfortable with his role as counselor when he began
to realize that he himself had so many unanswered questions.
"This fact," he later wrote, "affected not only my position as
dean of students but also my entire career. If I could offer little
real spiritual help to individuals, what did I have to offer the
state or the nation or the world?"[11]

Then, as a result of advising a student Bible study group,
things began to clarify themselves. He remembered his past
experiences: the loving care of his parents, his early reading of
the Bible, discussions in church about Jesus' call to commitment,

his assignment as a temporary chaplain during the war, and his experience of the Hiroshima aftermath. In retrospect he began to see the hand of God in his life. He was being brought to a turning point. Something very significant was about to happen.

It became increasingly obvious to Hatfield that his commitment to politics had not been matched by a commitment to Christ. Perhaps his religion, like his early successes in academia and politics, had come too easily. Perhaps he had not struggled long enough, and deep enough, with his relationship to God. He was on the brink of a new discovery, if only he could grasp what God had in mind for him.

Then, it all seemed to break loose. It was as if the floodgates had been opened, and it all finally poured out. Hatfield describes for us what happened.

. . . . I remember vividly the night in 1954 when it all came to a head. I was sitting alone in my room in my parents' home. For months my words in the classroom had been coming back to mock me. I was urging my students to stand up and be counted, but I was a very silent and very comfortable Christian. That night in the quiet of my room the choice was suddenly made clear. I could not continue to drift along as I had been doing, going to church because I had always gone, because everyone else went, because there wasn't any particular reason not to go. Either Christ was God and Savior and Lord or he wasn't; and if he were, then he had to have all my time, all my devotion, all my life.[12]

That evening in his parents' home Mark Hatfield committed his life to Christ. His decision to follow Christ was now firm; every area of his life would be dedicated to the declaration of God's love in Jesus Christ. In looking back on this moment, he has said, "I made the choice that night, many years ago; I *committed* myself to Christ. I saw that for thirty-one years I had lived for self, and I decided I wanted to live the rest of my life for Jesus Christ. I asked God to forgive my self-centeredness and to make me his own."[13]

In 1976 Senator Hatfield took a look back on his life since the time of his conversion to Christ. At this time he stated in a definitive way the new purpose of his life. "The purpose of my life," he wrote, "is to be faithful to Jesus Christ, to follow his way, and to be molded according to the imprint of his life."[14] Coming from some people, this sort of statement could have the hollow ring of a religious platitude—one which is spoken but not truly held. However, in the case of Mark Hatfield, his confession of faith has genuine integrity. This is because his deeds have been consistent with his words as he has sought to follow Jesus Christ as an advocate of God's peace in our world.

The Center of the Storm

One of the true ironies of the Christian life and the life of the peacemaker is that those who act in favor of peace often find themselves at the center of a storm of controversy. In Mark Hatfield's case the storm came with America's involvement in Vietnam. During the early 1960s he dared to speak out against a war which at that time had almost unanimous support among the American people. Large numbers of U.S. troops were yet to be committed to Southeast Asia, and it seemed reasonable to many Americans to "stop the spread of communism" in that part of the world.

Hatfield, however, had another perspective on Vietnam. He had been in Southeast Asia at the close of World War II. He had seen firsthand the terrible effects French colonialism had had upon the Vietnamese people. He understood the Vietnamese desire to be free of domination by the Western powers. After the Second World War he followed closely the political developments in Vietnam, and he could see a rising tide of nationalism within Vietnam. It was clear to Hatfield that by the end of the 1950s the United States had placed its support behind an unpopular government in Vietnam—a government without national support. He realized that our sole criterion in foreign policy was to help anybody who claimed to be "anti-Communist." In Hatfield's judgment this was an insufficient way to conduct foreign policy, and such policies based on an "anti-Communist" approach demonstrated a superficial grasp of complex political realities.[15]

As the keynote speaker at the Republican National Convention in 1964, Hatfield spoke out publicly against the war for the first time. He dared to question why we were in Vietnam. From the podium he asked: "Why, why do they [the Johnson Administration] fear telling the American people what our foreign policy is? Even when American boys are dying in a war without a name."[16] By 1966 the "war without a name" was heating up. Our nation had committed many more troops to the cause. In that year, at the Governors' Conference, a resolution was introduced to give blanket support to Johnson's war effort. Hatfield, then governor of Oregon, made it known that he in good conscience could not support the resolution.

It was a time of political crisis for Hatfield. Should he not support the resolution, the Democrats would say that he was making a partisan issue out of a matter of "national security." Likewise, his own party, the Republicans, would criticize him for grandstanding as a young party hopeful trying to make a name for himself in the national press. A number of the governors at the conference, Democrats and Republicans alike, counseled Hatfield *not* to vote against the resolution. They warned that if he did, he would be committing political suicide. (It was not wise to criticize the president on a foreign policy matter with troops already in the field.) When the vote was taken, it was forty-nine yes votes with only one no vote. Hatfield stood alone. He recalls that after the vote his wife, Antoinette, sent him "a note of love and pride and encouragement" from her seat in the observer's section of the conference.[17]

He had done what was right according to his conscience, but it would cost him dearly. He realized that he had placed his political future in jeopardy. In *Between a Rock and a Hard Place*, he characterized his situation in the following way:

> Politically I was a success, never having lost an election. As a young moderate Governor in the 1960s, the national press said I was "Presidential timber."
> Then the war came. My opposition was neither politically calculated nor strategically planned. It was intuitively, emotionally, from the depths.[18]

In the ensuing years Hatfield presented his position on Vietnam as a moral and spiritual issue. When he was elected to the United States Senate in 1967, most political analysts agreed that it was in spite of his Vietnam stand, and not because of it, that he won a seat in the Senate. As a senator, the former Oregon governor now had a truly national platform on which to argue his case against the war. This he did without hesitation.

The basis for Hatfield's opposition to the war was perhaps best expressed in a commencement speech given at Fuller Theological Seminary in 1970. He told the graduating class that their faith commitment to Christ needed to include an honest appraisal of world affairs. The gospel must be brought to bear against a nation's foreign policy. In the senator's words:

> As we consider the impact of Christ's gospel in these times, we must honestly confront the critical realities that characterize the life of the society and the world. . . .
> First and most obvious to us here in the United States is the war in Indochina. . . .
> I ask you to balance carefully and in good conscience evaluate the pros and cons to this endeavor and then have the courage to follow where your convictions lead you. Can we rationalize the human suffering, the wasted resources, and the deteriorization of moral sensitivity associated with this war supporting what seems to be an authoritarian puppet regime in Southeast Asia? Is the good to be achieved in this endeavor greater than the evil we are being forced to endure to achieve it?[19]

The graduating seminarians responded enthusiastically to Hatfield's message. However, much to his chagrin, many in the evangelical community questioned the senator's right even to call himself a Christian because of his unpatriotic opposition to the war.

Hatfield's witness for peace in Vietnam was also deemed unpatriotic by those in power at the White House. This was especially true during the Nixon years. The conflict between the Oregon senator and Nixon's people came to a climax as a result of the 1973 National Prayer Breakfast. By this time the war was close to being over, but Hatfield had lost none of his fire in opposing it. What troubled him most was the Nixon Administration's emphasis upon a "peace with honor." He could find little honor in a war which should never have been fought.

At the breakfast, Hatfield was scheduled as one of the speakers. It was perceived by most of Washington to be a perfunctory event—an opportunity to express a kind of national religiosity. However, Hatfield took the event quite seriously and he decided that he was going to speak his mind as a Christian layperson dedicated to peacemaking. During the breakfast he sat between his good friend Billy Graham and his political adversary Richard

Nixon. Cabinet members and congressional leaders sat at tables nearby. In *Between a Rock and a Hard Place*, the Senator has described the tensions which he felt within himself at that moment.

> I could not help but think, am I going to make a fool of myself before all these friends and associates? It was that feeling we all know which bids us to go along with the crowd, or not to risk doing something that may displease people whose friendship we deeply value. Those thoughts and feelings flashed through me.[20]

When Hatfield rose to speak, he called the nation to a time of repentance. His remarks were intended to humble a nation which seemed to want to avoid coming to grips with the tragedy of Vietnam. As he later recalled, "There was an overpowering impulse in America to believe that we had done no wrong— that we could come out of Indochina 'holding our heads up high.' This same spirit of haughty pride was echoed in the Administration at that time."[21] In part, the Senator's remarks are recorded here. His thoughts appear to be as timely for us today as when they were offered at the Prayer Breakfast a decade ago.

> We sit here today, as the wealthy and the powerful. But let us not forget that those who follow Christ will more often find themselves not with the comfortable majorities, but with the miserable minorities.
> Today, our prayers must begin with repentance. Individually, we must seek forgiveness for the exile of love from our hearts. And corporately as a people, we must turn in repentance from the sin that scarred our nation's soul.[22]

Hatfield concluded his remarks with a call for reconciliation; this was a plea many of the powerful leaders in the room had difficulty understanding.

> We must continually be transformed by Jesus Christ and take His commands seriously. Let us be Christ's messengers of reconciliation and peace, giving our lives over to the power of His love. Then we can soothe the wounds of war, and renew the face of the earth and all mankind.[23]

Once again Hatfield found himself at the center of a storm. The CBS Evening News showed clips of the Prayer Breakfast in which the Senator's comments were contrasted with the president's. The *New York Times* ran a story about the breakfast in which the headlines read, "Nixon Hears War Called a 'Sin.'" The White House took Hatfield's comments to be a personal attack upon the president. Rumors were spread to discredit the Oregon senator, and his name appeared on the "enemies list" of the Nixon White House staff. As with the other storms, Hatfield would also weather this one, and he would come out of it as dedicated to the task of peacemaking as he ever was—perhaps even stronger!

Shalom as a Way of Life

As we have seen in the life of Mark Hatfield, striving for peace is more than a passing phase in Christian discipleship. The one who follows Christ is asked to make the ministry of peace a lifetime vocation. Today, as many of us are aware, Senator Hatfield's continued commitment to peacemaking has made him a national leader in the grass-roots movement to reverse the arms race. His legislative efforts as an advocate of a nuclear freeze are a matter of public record. Perhaps more than any other person on Capitol Hill, he has consistently challenged the build-up of our nuclear arsenal.

For those who seek to follow Christ as peacemakers, it is important to understand the theological assumptions which undergird the peacemaking activities of Christians like Mark Hatfield. A careful investigation of what moves and motivates the senator in his lifetime dedication to peacemaking will help us establish our own spiritual commitment to the peace of Christ. It is evident by now that Hatfield's theological reflection on peacemaking begins with the Bible.

The Bible, in the senator's estimate, provides a mandate for peacemaking for those who hear its word. In the Old Testament he finds the concept of God's peace (shalom) to be most helpful. As Hatfield points out, biblical scholars have indicated that shalom is best defined not as the negation of war, but as the positive construction of harmonious relationships within God's created order. Shalom is the creation of wholeness; it is the establishment of justice in society and the promotion of love within our personal lives. It involves a commitment to the well-being of all God's creation.[24]

For Hatfield, the Old Testament concept of shalom is directly related to the New Testament life of Jesus. Jesus Christ is declared to be the Prince of Peace spoken about by the prophets when they envisioned the coming of God's shalom. In Christ we find the embodiment of God's peace in an unmistakable fashion. Therefore, those who choose to follow Jesus Christ can never divorce themselves from following in their Lord's ministry as a peacemaker. The Great Commandment to love God and love our neighbor (including our enemies) makes the requirements of Christian discipleship quite explicit.

In this regard, Hatfield's dedication to the way of shalom can be said to be based upon one basic theological assumption: God's entrance into the world through Jesus Christ was a call to peace, both in a personal and a social dimension. In Christ every barrier is broken down. This is true for the barriers we place between each other, and it is true for the barrier we establish between ourselves and God. Hatfield is fond of quoting the Phillips translation of Ephesians on this idea.

> He [Jesus Christ] has made a unity of the conflicting elements of Jew and Gentile by breaking down the barrier which lay between us. . . . and made in himself out of the two, Jew and Gentile, one new man, thus producing peace. For he reconciled both to God by the sacrifice of one body on the cross, and by this act made utterly irrelevant the antagonism between them. Then he came and told both you who were far from God and us who were near that the war was over (Ephesians 2:14-17, Phillips).[25]

In Hatfield's mind the war *is* truly over. We are neither Jew nor Greek, slave nor free, male nor female, but we are all one because of the love of God in Jesus Christ (see Galatians 3:26-29). This means that we are not to judge one another as Americans or Russians or Chinese. God does not categorize people according to nationality, or race, or ideology, or other such things. Christ has broken down all the barriers, and God intends that people live together in peace and justice.

But, we might protest, this is not the way the world is! Hatfield is very much aware of humanity's sinful state. He is enough of a realist to recognize that peacemaking will always be an uphill struggle. Yet it is essential that we hold onto the biblical concept of shalom. Actually, we can do none other since it is the way of our Lord. In this respect Hatfield becomes very impatient with fellow evangelicals who constantly remind him of our sinful nature. It is as if the doctrine of sin has been made more central to our faith than the doctrine of God's grace and mercy. Hatfield has lamented:

> When I discuss these matters [peacemaking] with some of my fellow Christians, they often claim that the reason we have no peace in the world is because of man's sin. As long as sin abounds, there will be "wars and rumors of wars," they say. I, of course, do not dispute the reality of man's selfish and sinful nature. But I do take issue with those who reject any responsibility for over-coming the obstacles to peace simply because sin is a reality. That was not the way of Christ. He has not told us that evil will ulti-mately triumph and that we should resign ourselves to such a fate. Rather, he asks that we follow him into the midst of man's turbulent world with his reconciling and redeeming love. Recognizing the existence of sin does not eliminate our mandate to act as peace-makers.[26]

Hatfield will not permit Christians to argue their way out of peacemaking.

Likewise, Hatfield views peacemaking as the task of every citizen. The alarming aspect of today's world is that the very word "peace" is disappearing from political dialogue. Most peo-ple are ignorant of the biblical concept of shalom; in addition, many of us do not even have a generalized notion of what makes for peace. This is evident in the rhetoric of our national security advisers. As Hatfield indicates, they fail to speak of the idea of peace altogether.

> . . . . They talk of increasing the probability of a world "that minimizes the incentives for armed, violent solutions to conflict situations." In other words, if there is anything one can call peace, it is the absence of war or violent conflict. This, I suspect, is the notion many of us share about the meaning of peace. It is estimated that the United States and the Soviet Union together possess ex-plosive power equivalent to fifteen tons of TNT for every person on the earth. Yet, many postulate that such a "balance of power" —or "balance of terror," to be more precise—is the only trust-worthy condition of peace.[27]

However, harking back to the biblical concept of shalom, Hatfield argues that there must be more positive alternatives to peacemaking than the making of more bombs to preserve a maddening "balance of terror."

The question for Hatfield is not whether we should have a strong national defense. He is willing to concede this point in our present political situation. The real question goes much deeper than our arguments about how many nuclear warheads are enough. The question as Hatfield sees it is "whether our trust rests solely in our military power as a means of insuring our security and peace."[28] If it does, then the senator believes we are in big trouble. Those who follow the biblical mandate for peacemaking know that reliance upon military might is no true guarantee of peace. Quoting from the prophet, Hosea, Hatfield reminds us, "Because you have trusted in your chariots and in the multitude of your warriors, therefore the tumult of war shall arise among your people (Hosea 10:13-14).

What Is Peace?

What, then, can be said? Have we already passed the point of no return? Have we lost any hope for peace since we no longer have any notion of its meaning? The answer would be yes, except for one unrelenting factor. We still know of the existence of peacemakers—persons like Mark Hatfield who keep a vision of peace alive. Should we, like the senator, desire to express our peacemaking through a Christian witness, then we would do well to consider what his life teaches us.

First, we must realize that peace is an empty word without a personal commitment to peacemaking. As with Hatfield, we need to learn that peace is an active verb rather than a static noun. When Jesus said, "Blessed are the peacemakers," the emphasis was upon discovering for ourselves the things which make for peace both within and without. When we ask about peace, we are really asking what it takes for us to be peacemakers. Like the Christian faith, peacemaking requires of its advocates a total commitment.

Second, we should be aware that the ministry of peacemaking will probably place us at the center of a storm of controversy. Like Mark Hatfield, we may find that our peace stance will draw critical responses from others. In many cases we should be prepared to deal with opposition to our peacemaking from within the Christian community. As Hatfield discovered, our greatest opponents may very well be our brothers and sisters in Christ who are convinced that we have misread the gospel. In addition, the Christian peacemaker, like other peacemakers, should be ready for personal charges of "unpatriotic behavior" which will come from those who believe it is an act of treason to question our nation's intentions in foreign affairs. There will be an inevitable clash of values with those in our world who find peacemaking to be too idealistic for the "real" world. Here we can take comfort in the knowledge that Jesus confronted similar opposition. Peacemakers are perceived by many as dangerous individuals, and some are even crucified.

In the third place, we can discover with Senator Hatfield that peacemaking brings great joy. In spite of the constant uphill climb, there is something basically life-affirming about peacemaking. Those who work for peace in the name of Christ know that they stand with a resurrected Lord. The last word is not war and destruction; the last word is peace. In various accounts of Jesus' own resurrection, it is reported that he greeted his followers with a word of *peace*.

Finally, we ought to recognize with Hatfield that our peacemaking efforts cannot be sustained without a clear understanding of our motives. The senator's commitment to peace is firmly grounded in his own theology and spirituality. He is a peacemaker because he believes that peace is what God intends for creation. In this sense, peacemaking embraces the breadth and depth of all that concerned Jesus; the pursuit of God's shalom involves a witness for the total spiritual and physical well-being of humanity. To be a Christian means to be an advocate for peace.

Therefore, against all odds, we are called to be peacemakers. As with Mark Hatfield, our dedication to God's shalom cannot ultimately rest upon our own estimates as to whether peace is a "realistic" goal. Our commitment is based on another sort of hope. Out of the challenge to follow Christ, we must come to realize that our most important reason for peacemaking is Jesus

Christ himself. God, through Christ, continues to call us to be makers of peace, and with God's help we must persist. Someday we all may come to know and truly grasp the meaning of God's shalom. Until then we will do well to consider the challenge for peace which Senator Hatfield has set before us.

So we go forth into the world seeking new possibilities, grasping God's vision of what he can do. We have the certain hope that he can impart new life—new life to individuals, to nations, and to all creation. That hope is based in the Risen Christ. All history is consummated in him. He is our Peace.[29]

Recommended Readings

Mark Hatfield

Not Quite So Simple. New York: Harper & Row, Publishers, Inc., 1968.

Conflict and Conscience. Waco, Texas: Word Books, 1971.

Between a Rock and a Hard Place. Waco, Texas: Word Books, 1977.

NOTES

[1]This information was gathered from an interview with Mark Hatfield in June, 1983, in Salem, Oregon.
[2]Mark Hatfield, *Conflict and Conscience* (Waco, Texas: Word Books, 1971), p. 154.
[3]*Ibid.*, p. 153.
[4]*Ibid.*, p. 155.
[5]*Ibid.*, p. 94.
[6]Hatfield interview, June, 1983.
[7]Hatfield interview, June, 1983.
[8]Hatfield, *Conflict and Conscience*, p. 95.
[9]Mark Hatfield, *Not Quite So Simple* (New York: Harper & Row, Publishers, Inc., 1968), p. 9.
[10]Hatfield, *Conflict and Conscience*, p. 96.
[11]*Ibid.*, p. 97.
[12]*Ibid.*, p. 98.
[13]*Ibid.*
[14]Mark Hatfield, *Between a Rock and a Hard Place* (Waco, Texas: Word Books, 1976), p. 26.
[15]Hatfield, *Not Quite So Simple*, pp. 258-267.
[16]*Ibid.*, pp. 155–156.
[17]*Ibid.*, p. 161.
[18]Hatfield, *Between a Rock and a Hard Place*, p. 22.
[19]Hatfield, *Conflict and Conscience*, p. 28.

[20] Hatfield, *Between a Rock and a Hard Place*, p. 93.
[21] *Ibid.*, pp. 92-93.
[22] *Ibid.*, p. 94.
[23] *Ibid.*, p. 95.
[24] Hatfield, *Conflict and Conscience*, p. 40.
[25] *Ibid.*, p. 44.
[26] *Ibid.*, pp. 40-41.
[27] *Ibid.*, p. 39.
[28] *Ibid.*, p. 48.
[29] *Ibid.*, p. 50.

8

What Are the Marks of the Christian Life?

He called the people and the disciples to him and said, "If anyone wants to be a follower of mine, let him renounce himself and take up his cross and follow me. For anyone who wants to save his life will lose it; but anyone who loses his life for my sake, and for the sake of the gospel will save it.
—Mark 8:34-35 (Jerusalem Bible)

What are the marks of the Christian life? Having carefully examined the life and thought of various contemporary Christians, it is now time to summarize the lessons we have learned from "so great a cloud of witnesses." We need to chart the course of our Christian lives for the future. Certainly, we have come to understand that the way of faith in any generation is not an easy road to travel. As Elizabeth O'-Connor has pointed out, we are invited by Jesus Christ to take the way of the narrow gate. In fact, in each voice which has spoken to us we have heard the distant echo of Jesus himself: "For anyone who wants to save his life will lose it; but anyone who loses his life for my sake, and for the sake of the gospel will save it."

We have learned that the life of faith is built upon one major paradox. Should we be concerned about our own salvation (a question which did not preoccupy our witnesses), we are placing ourselves in a position to lose everything. On the other hand, should we give up our concern for personal gain (something our witnesses did do), we are locating ourselves on the road to

redemption and new life. Hence, any discussion of the Christian
life must keep in mind that the living of a faithful life cannot be
an end in itself. We seek a faithful Christian existence not for
personal reward but for service of our Lord and the kingdom
he proclaimed.

Following Jesus Christ, we must be prepared to take up our
crosses. The women and men we have studied on these pages
have identified many modern struggles which require the commitment of Christ's followers. In the name of Jesus they have
challenged everything from fascism to racism to sexism to ma-
terialism to militarism. They have taken up the cross of protest
against many forces in life which dehumanize us. Our witnesses
have encouraged us not to turn our backs on the world's burdens
which we are called to bear in the liberating name of Jesus Christ.

In this regard our witnesses have grounded their lives in the
power and vitality of Christ's Spirit. Whether they have spoken
to us of our inward journey to God or our outward life of moral
commitment, the model for faithfulness has been Jesus of Nazareth. Throughout this study we have been exposed to the
fundamental conviction that the focus of faith for the Christian
must be Jesus. The Christian life begins and ends with Jesus
Christ; there is simply no other way to be Christian than to
follow Jesus. Unless our Christian lives are infused with the
living reality of Christ, they will wither and die like a branch
cut off from its main trunk. Howard Thurman's childhood experience of Jesus under the oak tree in his backyard is a powerful
image for the foundational quality of Jesus Christ for the Christian life. Jesus Christ, the mighty oak, is indeed present for us
in our growth and development as his followers. To state the
matter categorically, Jesus Christ will truly be present for us in
the struggles we pass through in his name.

A Committed Life

The Christian life, a life lived in Christ, is a committed life.
As Dietrich Bonhoeffer demonstrated so forcefully, we cannot
really know Jesus Christ unless we are prepared to pay the cost
of discipleship. Christ did not become real for Bonhoeffer until
he was able to make the shift from Bonhoeffer the theologian

(the man of ideas) to Bonhoeffer the Christian (the man of action). His commitment to challenge Adolf Hitler and Nazism, like the commitments of Helder Camara and Mark Hatfield to be peacemakers, was also a commitment to Jesus Christ. In the Christian life we are called to make our commitments in the real world—the world in which we can get hurt, the world in which we can be crushed. Bonhoeffer recognized that Christians for too long had committed themselves to trivial matters which had no real impact on the world. However, the call to commitment is a call to give our entire life to Christ. We are to hold nothing back; Christ informs every aspect of our life in the world.

Another way of speaking about the committed Christian life is to say that a commitment to Jesus Christ is a commitment to his kingdom. However, many of us who seek to follow Christ never make it to the point of kingdom commitment. We are willing to follow Jesus Christ to the extent that we worship him as Lord and Savior, but we are reluctant to follow Christ to the extent that we work for his kingdom, a kingdom defined as God's shalom. We are speaking once again about the narrow gate. Christ calls us to live in faith; we are to trust that the kingdom which Jesus proclaimed is actually emerging in our life and the life of the world, even when "facts" suggest the opposite.

We have every incentive to follow the crowd through the broad gate. We know we will be rewarded for not rocking the boat. We will be accepted; we will be praised, and chances are we will be exceedingly bored! The real challenge is in the narrow gate. In following Jesus, we are confronted by the unknown. We are asked to take risks and we are encouraged not to accept the leveling values of the world. It is true: the life committed to Christ has no direct rewards. Christ does not call us to victory, but he does call us to discipleship; we can find our joy in a life of service to others.

Our life of commitment will result in conflict. Without exception, the lives of the witnesses we have examined evidence stormy conflicts. This would not be commendable if the conflicts were simply a function of troublesome personalities; however, the cases we have studied reveal another type of conflict—a conflict which results from faith commitments. In this regard, our lives would be far less complicated and turbulent if we did not commit them to God's gospel. However, should we choose to live a committed Christian life, then we must be prepared for the uncomfortable reality of value clashes. Our adoption of Jesus' values will place us in jeopardy with many of the world's values. As Howard Thurman has suggested to us, Jesus' values sided with the poor and the oppressed. He favored the rights of the poor over unfair laws and insensitive institutions. Should we truly identify with those on the bottom of life as Jesus did, then we will undoubtedly make those on the top quite angry. Should we challenge the idea of male domination in life, then we can expect a backlash from those who do not share in the belief that we are all equal in God's eyes. And so it goes. The Christian life is at every step a potential confrontation.

The life of commitment, however, is not all conflict. Commitment to the cause of Jesus Christ also results in a sense of lasting peace. We recognize through our commitment that we are "in it for the long run." The Christian life cannot be lived as a fad or a passing fancy. It is not a product to be bought, used, and then discarded. In the Christian life we find ourselves enveloped in a reality which gains greater and greater depth. We want to give more and more of ourselves to it. The immature might complain: "I'm not getting anything out of this," but the mature follower of Christ will ask: "What more can I put into this?"

There is indeed a profound sense of accomplishment which comes with our commitment to Christ. Simply to be able to say that "I did what I set out to do" and to be able to recognize that "I stuck with it" yields tremendous satisfaction in our society which is so fixated on immediate gratification. Commitment to Jesus Christ is commitment for a lifetime. Like the marriage contract, we expect this commitment to be a lasting one. In this respect we must be willing to forego the "cheap grace" of which Bonhoeffer spoke, for the sake of true discipleship. Our commitment must be grounded in a determination to live the life of "costly grace."

A Spiritual Life

In the second place, the Christian life is marked by a commitment to a personal spirituality. Howard Thurman's focus upon the religion *of* Jesus should serve as a reminder for us not to forget that life cannot be whole without an intimate sense of being related to God. Just as Jesus' entire life was filled with an awareness of God's presence, so too should our lives be illuminated by the light of God. When it comes to our spirituality, there can be no such thing as a secondhand believer. Life in the Spirit can make sense only if it is *our* life in the Spirit.

Many Christians have avoided the inner life of the spirit because they are embarrassed by what they perceive to be the emotionalism of spirit-filled individuals. Granted, we all know of spiritual exhibitionists, that is, people who try to impress others with their piety and spiritual devotion. But the shallow "Praise God" mentality is nothing new. As Jesus demonstrated, it was a problem among the Pharisees of his day. Nevertheless, we must be ready to embrace the word "spiritual" as an important indicator of our commitment to an interior life of faith.

For the Christian, the living of a spiritual life coincides with the theological recognition that the Creator of the universe is identical with the God of the Bible. At its heart, Christian spirituality affirms the living God of Abraham and Sarah, and of Jesus Christ. As Carlyle Marney has indicated, philosophers have argued about the existence of God, but biblical people have existed in relationship to the living Lord—and so it is for the follower of Christ today. This does not mean that our spiritual lives are free from questions. Quite the contrary is true. Because we have a personal relationship with God, the questions become even more complex and they take on all the dynamics of a personal encounter.

However, despite all our questions, there remains a basic conviction that God is indeed present for us. Where others may find God to be absent, people of faith uncover the movement of God's Spirit. In this respect, Howard Thurman was able to experience a living God in spite of the racist environment of his childhood. Archbishop Camara, another spiritually sensitive individual, was able to discover God in the faces of Brazilian

peasants who lived in abject poverty. Similarly, Virginia Mollenkott could find God in a Bible which her church said was for
men only. And so it goes. Those who are open to their own
spiritual longings are able to find God in places where others
find only emptiness and disappointment.

Likewise, those who seek to live close to God are strengthened
by the exercise of spiritual disciplines. The spiritual person must
be alert to the disciplines which will best serve his or her own
needs for growth. Our witnesses all sought their own pathways
to God. Some emphasized prayer. Following the lead of Jesus'
life, many of our witnesses have turned aside from daily activities to find a quiet place. Prayer is cultivated as a means of
sensing God's presence and God's will. As Thurman has taught,
the practice of prayer does not mean finding an effective way
to get God's ear; rather, it means discovering new ways to listen
to what God might be saying to us. The use of silence in a world
filled with clamor is perhaps the most essential spiritual discipline for our times.

Recovering a life in the Spirit also means a renewed commitment to simplicity. We have learned from our witnesses that
simplicity may be the major hallmark of the Christian life for
the future. Camara's commitment to simplicity as a sign of his
identification with the poor of the earth is a genuine challenge
for us. Bonhoeffer's prediction that the future of Christianity
would be marked by only two things, "prayer and righteous
action," deserves further consideration. In a time of dwindling
resources, we may need to declare that material affluence is an
affront to Christ's gospel. Simplicity is not an alternative life-
style for the Christian: it is *the* life-style for Christians.

A Prophetic Life

In addition to the challenge of the Christian life to recover our
own spirituality, there is also the call to live a public life of faith.
This third mark of the Christian life is called the prophetic
witness. Some have balked at the idea that the prophetic witness
is for all Christians. It is true that we are not all called to be Old
Testament prophets, but Jesus did challenge each of us to be
proclaimers of God's emerging kingdom. This kingdom is a

prophetic kingdom of peace and justice. Indeed, almost any social issue in our time can be addressed by means of these two great prophetic themes. Our witnesses have indicated that it is the responsibility of every Christian to carry the themes of God's justice and peace into a world filled with injustice and war.

Unfortunately, our American brand of Christianity plays the prophetic notes of the Bible in a minor key. Precisely at the moment when we should be most prophetic, we seem to have lost all prophetic vision. Many of us no longer dream dreams; we no longer ask why things cannot be as Jesus envisioned them in the Sermon on the Mount. We have lost our idealism, and we have failed to challenge our young people to prophetic witness. The hard truth is that we have met the enemy and it is us! To exercise a prophetic ministry in our time might mean to open ourselves to self-criticism.

We have become too comfortable. The self-righteous attitudes of our national life betray an arrogance which fashions our country as a "chosen nation." We are not a chosen nation! Far too often we have failed to make the moral connections between our own affluence and the world's poverty. We are rich Christians in a hungry world. To be sure, our life in this affluent culture is an accident of birth. Over this "blessing" we have little control, but we can be responsible for how we choose to handle our privileged positions. Do we as Christians seek to share wealth and power with others for their empowerment? Are we willing to lower our standard of living so that others might experience something other than subhuman living conditions? These are questions which the follower of Christ must confront in our time of prophetic judgment.

Several of our witnesses have argued for a change in our social consciousness. In our Christian life, consciousness raising is akin to the prophet's cry for repentance. When Jesus called for his generation to repent, was he not calling for a complete reorientation of our world perspective? In this regard, our conversion in Jesus Christ includes not only a personal commitment to Christ's Spirit, but also a social commitment to Christ's world— the world which God created and sustains. A commitment to Jesus Christ is a commitment to view all things differently. As

Bonhoeffer suggested, we are called to see life "from below." Helder Camara referred to this kind of conversion as the adoption of a new consciousness, a consciousness which allows us to view life from the perspective of the oppressed rather than the oppressor.

Yet this change in consciousness is far more than an ideological shift. The social and political worlds are not the only things to be viewed differently. As in the thought of Howard Thurman, we are called to view our very selves differently—as children of God. We are to find God's Spirit in every human being to the end that no individual or group can be dehumanized, because an attack upon any of us is an attack upon God. Fortunately we do have a norm for this new consciousness and that is Christ Jesus. This means that our strategies for prophetic calls to conversion must be developed in a Christlike manner. Our call for peace and justice needs to be consistent with our understanding of Jesus' call for peace and justice. Among our witnesses, Helder Camara and Howard Thurman made this point with great force. Regardless of what others might do or say, the Christian approach to social transformation must be a nonviolent one. Loving confrontation may be a part of responsible Christian living, but the overt use of violence can never be justified on the basis of Christ's gospel. Violence might be unavoidable in some situations; however, it can never be honored by any sort of Christian justification. Camara is correct in his assertion that violence only breeds more violence. As Christians we are called to say no to violence, and in so doing we are asked to recognize the way our own affluence has perpetuated violence. We must reject the violence of our own wealth and position, and we must resist the violence of our city streets and war zones.

Above all else it is important for the Christian to realize that the prophetic aspect of our Christian life is not all gloom and doom. Living a prophetic life can open us to believers of other religions. We recognize through our social action that Christians are not the only ones concerned about peace and justice. Many Buddhists, Hindus, Muslims, and Jews share in our prophetic concern for world harmony. Only our own spiritual arrogance keeps us from seeing the many ways in which God can work through the lives of "non-Christians." When we are secure in our own spiritual journeys, we discover the great joy of sharing life with other people of good will around the world. Certainly we do not all confess Jesus as Lord, but we do share in a common commitment to God's shalom—a reality to which Jesus also pointed. The prophetic thrust to affirm and protect the dignity of all God's children will carry us far beyond the boundaries of our Christian communities.

A Community Life

There is a sense, however, in which the basis of our Christian life has to remain the church. A fourth mark of the Christian life involves our commitment to a community of faith. There is no way around the simple truth that we need a place to grow in Jesus Christ, and that place is Christ's church. Granted, many of us are dissatisfied with the church as an institution. Indeed, several of our witnesses criticized the church and worked for its renewal. The church *is* in deep trouble. It is very close to losing its reason for being. It seems to lack a genuine commitment to Jesus Christ and the kingdom of God. However, the church remains the only visible institution which celebrates Christ's presence in the world, no matter how inadequately this is done!

We are aware of the church's failures. Bonhoeffer attacked the Nazi-dominated German Protestant Church. Marney rejected the American version of the institutional church. Thurman even created a new kind of church—an inclusive, integrated congregation. At almost every point our witnesses held out for a grander vision for the church.

Perhaps Elizabeth O'Connor came closest to the real problem with the contemporary church when she suggested that many of our congregations are spiritually bankrupt. She insisted that for the church to be the church, it must be gathered in the name of Jesus Christ. We cannot know what we are to do as a church until we understand who we are. Therefore, O'Connor and the Church of the Saviour suggest the journey inward-journey outward. Until the church, in its membership, is dedicated to each member's commitment to mission and ministry, it will remain an institution dominated by professionals who are hired to do the job every Christian ought to be doing. In truth, the church can be renewed only when the "priesthood of all believers" is once again emphasized.

The church is indeed a very human institution, and it can be accused of hypocrisy, wishy-washy tendencies, and all the rest. It is true that many of our main-line Protestant churches have faded into the landscape of our American way of life often it is difficult to distinguish the church from other voluntary organizations such as the Lion's Club or the Rotary. In fact there is little "protest" remaining in American Protestantism. Even more to the point, there may be little "Christian" left in Christianity.

The recovery of Christ's church is on the agenda of most Christian groups today. And almost everybody agrees that the renewal of the church depends upon a new commitment to Christ as the head of the church. But the real question is, What kind of a Christ are we talking about? Or as Bonhoeffer expressed it, Who is Christ for us today? This is the most important debate in the church today. Along with Bonhoeffer we would argue that the real Jesus Christ must be met as personal Lord and Savior and as the Servant of the world. In the final analysis we need to recover Christ's centrality for the church so that we can once again discover his centrality for the world. If we cannot find Christ in the sharing of our joys and sorrows within the Christian fellowship, we certainly will not be able to find Christ's presence in the world.

A Frontier Life

A fifth mark of the Christian life is our frontier existence. We are not only called into the church, we are also called to explore the unknown. Like Jesus, we are to press beyond the boundaries which have been imposed upon us—boundaries of race, creed, and religion. We are called to live on the cutting edge; like Jesus, we are to challenge the "sacred cows" of our society. We are to champion the right of each child of God to think for himself or herself. In this sense, the actions of our Christian lives will draw us toward a broader and more inclusive understanding of life— one in which prejudice, arrogance, and spiritual bigotry knows no place.

As Christians, we acknowledge that our world faces many new frontiers. These modern frontiers have very little to do with geographic boundaries or foreign lands; they involve new horizons of morality and spirituality. Bonhoeffer, for example, had to chart a new ethical path in order to confront Nazism. By pushing back the frontiers of faith, Bonhoeffer dared to be different. Senator Hatfield's decision to follow his Christian conscience on the issue of Vietnam is another example of pushing back the frontiers of faith. He knew that his opposition to the Southeast Asia war would cost him his chance at the presidency, but he persisted in challenging the government's foreign policy because he believed it was morally wrong.

Again and again our witnesses were willing to live on the frontiers of faith because their inclusive understanding of life drew them to ever greater horizons. When Howard Thurman decided to pursue his interests in mysticism, he knew he would be in uncharted waters. He understood that he was crossing into territory many Christians considered taboo. However, the truth of God's presence in his own life could not be ignored. In the spirit of Jesus himself, Thurman knew he must be free to go where God was leading him. Similarly, Dom Helder Camara's decision to side with the poor of Brazil placed him in uncharted territory for a Roman Catholic bishop. Most bishops in Brazil sided with the status quo of their country's landed aristocracy. Dom Helder knew that his frontier excursion could cost him his reputation and even his life. Nevertheless, he persisted because he understood the gospel as a challenge to live as Jesus lived, as a challenge to identify with the oppressed and the disenfranchised. All of our witnesses have known that to follow Jesus means to be a frontier person. Boundaries of race, sex, social position, and nationality meant nothing to Jesus; therefore, they have had no meaning for our witnesses. Those who follow Jesus mark off new sets of coordinates which are broad enough to embrace the boundless grace of God.

Living on the frontier of faith requires that we not be afraid to be different. All of our witnesses had features in their personalities which made them memorable. We should not be afraid to be "characters." We should not be afraid to stand out in the crowd. Far too often we have operated with the assumption that it is okay to be Christian so long as we do not draw attention to ourselves. Perhaps it is time to be different, as was Christ.

A Joyous Life

A final mark of the Christian life is joy. This too we share with our Lord, Jesus Christ. From a Christian perspective it is safe to say that our commitment, our spiritual journey, our prophetic witness, our life together, and our frontier faith are all empty gestures without the presence of joy. Like the early followers of Jesus, we need to reflect the tremendous joy and zest for life which was a part of their resurrection faith. We are not referring to the plaster-faced smile or the glad-handing which often passes for Christianity; we are speaking rather of a deep fountain of peace whose source is the living Christ.

As in the life of Jesus, this joy cannot be contained. It overflows into every corner of our lives. The joy of Christ is marked by a childlike willingness to laugh and play in God's creation. With this attitude the most simple events in life can become occasions for life's celebration. In this regard some of our witnesses have helped us recover a sense of true joy in the experiences of the natural world. Others have helped us rediscover the warmth of human personality and the love of intimate relationships. We need to remember that although our witnesses took life seriously, they never took themselves too seriously.

Without question we are confronted by many serious problems in the world today. We live in somber times; we are aware of the human capacity to end it all in one tremendous nuclear holocaust. These are times which call for creative and compassionate solutions to our global problems. However, in the midst of all this chaos, we must not forget the joy of our faith—a faith which is grounded in an awareness that God continues to love us and act in our world. God's word to us in Jesus Christ is that we do not have to accept the world's ways. We do not have to share in its pessimism and despair. We can stand for love, we can work for justice, and we can be peacemakers. Jesus Christ has freed us to do all of this and more. The challenges for living a responsible moral and spiritual life are always before us, and the good news is that we can truly be faithful to this challenge because of Jesus. He is our joy as Christians! He is our life.

Index